Prisoner in Al-Khobar:
A true story about the life of an expatriate in the eastern province of Saudi Arabia during the 1990s

D. A. Norman

Clink Street

London | New York

Published by Clink Street Publishing 2018

Copyright © 2018

First edition.

The author asserts the moral right under the Copyright, Designs and Patents Act 1988 to be identified as the author of this work.

All rights reserved. No part of this publication may be reproduced, stored in a retrieval system or transmitted, in any form or by any means without the prior consent of the author, nor be otherwise circulated in any form of binding or cover other than that with which it is published and without a similar condition being imposed on the subsequent purchaser.

ISBN:
978-1-912562-35-0 - paperback
978-1-912562-36-7 - ebook

Dedication to Sharon, patient as always.

Contents

Part 1

Chapter 1:	Come to the Gulf	3
Chapter 2:	The Sponsor & the Show	7
Chapter 3:	Joint Venture	15
Chapter 4:	New Boys	25
Chapter 5:	Finding My Feet	31
Chapter 6:	Spring	45
Chapter 7:	Get Me Out Of Here	59
Chapter 8:	Summer	71

Part 2

Chapter 9:	Come Again?	85
Chapter 10:	Bahrain	99
Chapter 11:	Join Forces	109
Chapter 12:	Aramco	123
Chapter 13:	All Over the Place	137

Part 3

Chapter 14:	Come Together	151
Chapter 15:	West and North	165
Chapter 16:	Out and About	171
Acknowledgements		187

D. A. Norman

Part 1

Chapter 1

Come to the Gulf

If you're bored with your day to day working life, be careful what you wish for. That's how I was feeling. So, if you ever consider selling your soul please remember it's the devil getting it back. I don't think I actually sold my soul, well I hope not, but I know I wanted something more in my working life.

Well, I reckon that's what happened to me when the phone on my desk rang in the middle of September in 1994. I knew the caller and he asked if I would be interested in exhibiting at a trade show in Saudi Arabia.

He lived and worked there and saw an opportunity to make a lot of money. Apparently, the products I was dealing with were quite new to the region and they would go down a storm; not a desert storm, I hoped. He said it would be easy to sell to the Arabs and a fortune could be made. Oh yes, I had problems selling to the English, let alone Arabs. Anyway. I fell for it as pound signs flicked through my brain and I agreed to go. I'd been stuck in the office for a while and wanted something exciting to happen and this sounded like it. My biggest problem was that my bank balance was very low and I couldn't put much into the deal. My partners at the time were sceptical and didn't want to waste time or money on a fool's errand. Well, I now know that I was that fool, but I wasn't deterred so I started planning it myself. Naivety was an understatement but in for a penny, which is about all I had, in for a pound, a few of which is what I hoped to make. I had no idea of the complex nature of a trip to Saudi Arabia. Firstly, you need a sponsor. What a palaver; I mean, I've travelled quite a lot on business trips including a couple of times to Abu Dhabi in the UAE, and never needed one before.

Well, the guy who started all this had an idea about that and asked an Arab friend of his to act as my sponsor in return for a cut of the deal.

This Arab friend was a business man who owned a cement company and was willing to 'look after me' during my stay. The first thing I needed was to arrange a visit visa. I had to fax a photocopy of my passport to the sponsor and he would send it to the Saudi Arabian embassy in London stating he needed me to visit him for a business deal, which in a sense was true because I thought I was only going to be there for a week. So, I had to take my passport to the Saudi Embassy and they would verify the copy and issue a thirty day visa. My mate in Saudi had told me my new sponsor had loads of contacts and one would meet me at the airport. So, he's got a few mates too, I thought; I had no idea how many he had.

So I caught a Gulf Air flight from Heathrow Airport to Dhahran in Saudi Arabia with fifty quid and a Diners Club card in my pocket. We took off in the afternoon and landed in the morning but I'd slept most of the way so I had the illusion of time travel.

I was looking forward to a nice little break in the sunshine, especially in October, so I was thinking it was not a bad temperature first thing in the morning. It was the end of their summer season, which lasts from May to October. As that first day wore on though I found out there's plenty of sunshine, and you end up searching for shade very quickly.

To my surprise my guy was waiting for me by the steps of the plane near the entrance to the terminal. We walked out of the sun's heat into the air-conditioned chill of the terminal. The terminal was new and very big, pale fabricated stone and tinted glass panels. A man stood just inside the door. He had a wide brimmed hat, a big belly, a damp cigar end, brown eyes and an air of authority. He was a dynastic man and this was his domain. He steered me wide of the crowd of passengers heading towards passport control. There were two queues, a very small one for Saudi nationals and a massive one for everyone else.

I didn't know how but we bypassed the queues, but he steered me through a side door to the front of the queue. I wasn't sure whether to feel privileged or scared. My bags were waiting and I was in, or so I thought.

Saudi Arabian customs is entirely different to any I'd had the privilege to pass through before. Every bag is opened and everything in them is inspected. I had brought some thriller/crime novels and the customs officer asked me what they were about and when I said I didn't know because I hadn't read them yet they were confiscated. I saw a guy in the queue before me explaining why he had photos of his infant child. Thank the lord I didn't have any rude magazines or I'd have been carted away.

It was extremely hot, by the way.

***

I'd looked up Dhahran and this is what I found out. It is in the eastern province of Saudi Arabia and a major administrative center for the Saudi oil industry; it's home to a major base of Royal Saudi Air Force and the most prestigious Saudi university, KFUPM. Together with the nearby cities of Ad Dammam and Al-Khobar, Dhahran forms part of the Dammam Metropolitan Area, which is commonly known as greater Dammam.

Together, they are often known as 'The Triplet Cities' by many natives and locals. Dammam, Dhahran and Al-Khobar are less than 15km (9.3mi) apart and form one metropolitan area, the fifth largest in the kingdom and sixth in the Gulf Cooperation Council.

***

The show was in Al-Khobar, where I would be staying for the week.

Chapter 2

The Sponsor & the Show

Saud

It's 50 km from the terminal to Al-Khobar city, about 30 miles, with desert on both sides of the road. We went straight to my new sponsor's office, where I was introduced to him. When I first met Saud Al-Harbi I wasn't sure what to make of him but was soon impressed. I saw a man who looked in total control of his life. He looked about my age but he was in fact an astonishingly youthful forty-eight. He had black hair, just a little gray over his ears with a long narrow face, deeply seamed and a thin lipped mouth with a small twisted smile which looked habitual. He was dressed in a white dishdasha and looked very cool. There was a massive fan on full blast just behind him standing in the corner, while I was a bit hot under the collar in my suit and tie. He seemed relaxed, watchful and reasonably friendly.

He clicked his fingers and his 'tea-boy' came in and asked if I would like some tea. Elevenses sounded nice so tea all round then, got any biscuits? Saud sat at his desk and looked down on me like a solicitor on his elevated chair and I felt like a person he could control. I had one of those strange moments of unreality, that old 'what-am-I-doing-here' feeling.

'Get control of yourself or go home' was going through my mind. The moment passed and the tea came, on a silver tray mind you, with a glass of water each. There was no milk, just black tea in a very small glass with loads of sugar. I was glad of the water.

There was another guy sitting smoking in the corner who Nick, my contact, told me was Saud's translator if we needed one. Saud badly needed one but he wanted to show me he was in charge and tried his best to speak to me in English. He couldn't speak much English but enough to make me understand he wanted us to work together for a long time.

Maybe it was his accent or his pigeon English but the way he said the word 'long' unnerved me.

Saud's company made and sold concrete, and had absolutely nothing to do with the computer hardware and software I was dealing with. Never mind, I thought, he would be just a sleeping partner in this new venture. How wrong could I be? He asked me to refer to him as Mr. Saud and I was Mr. Dennis. A great start, already on first name basis.

Saud was the type of person who breezed through life and who thought, like me, he could make some money from the arrangement.

Three wives and a few children seemed a perfectly natural result of his controlled energy.

So he had gone along with Nick and agreed to sponsor me. It was only a week for me to exhibit at the trade show anyway, so it wouldn't cost him much.

His company was ticking along nicely with no problems and he didn't have to do much. His staff ran it and he just popped in a few times a week to get away from all those wives.

So he was OK with me doing all the work. Anyway, I liked the guy and I thought I'd start calling myself Mr. Dennis Al Norman. So from then on I signed that on all my correspondence. London office thought it was a joke until I explained my middle name is actually Allan.

Seaview

After the meeting Nick invited me to his place to meet his wife and daughter. They lived in a really nice villa on a compound called Seaview. What's a compound, I heard myself saying? The dictionary says it's 'a group of residences set off and enclosed by a barrier'. Basically, in Saudi Arabia it's a place which is enclosed by barbed wire to keep people out and in.

'To keep the religious police out,' Nick said.

'Whoa, why do you need to keep them out, Nick?'

'So we can have a drink,' he chuckled.

How I needed a drink in this heat nobody knows. Nick wanted a Jack Daniels. Don't ask me how he smuggled whiskey into Saudi, I had no idea at the time; all I wanted was a long glass of water, or even a cold beer, with plenty of ice. It's over thirty five degrees out there. Still, it had been a long night and an even longer day, plus the time difference of four hours, so I longed to freshen up and relax. Nick went back to work. Kaitlin was fussing over me offering me this and that, but after an eight hour overnight flight I was ready for bed so I dozed for a couple of hours in the spare room. The temperature didn't drop that much as evening came. I went to the pool for a dip but even that didn't cool me down, the water had been warmed all day by the sun and it was like a warm bath. No chance of an early night either – Nick and Kaitlin wanted to know what had been happening in England, so we sat up till late and talked. No rush to get to work tomorrow, I thought, but there was a show to prepare for. I had assumed Nick had some idea what we needed to build a stand at a trade show. He had been to a few but only as a visitor. I'd done a few myself but I had partners in London and they knew a thing or two. Problem was, they weren't here, and I was on my own.

Nick and Saud

Nick had met Saud at a company party. It was something to do with the oil industry and Saud had been invited because his company had been a supplier in a new office they had just built. Nick is your typical Scotsman and noticed a bottle of whiskey being offered around. Considering Saudi Arabia has a complete ban on alcohol he obviously wanted some, but more than that, he wanted to know how to get some more. It is illegal to produce it, import it, or consume it but sometimes it was smuggled in. He asked around and was introduced to a couple of guys who knew a few more who could get some. Saud's translator was listening in and as he was Saud's right hand man, he was there to get things for Saud and make sure all was well with him. The translator was called Mosem and he agreed to keep this information secret as long as nothing would come back to bite him. So another friendship started.

Mosem was Egyptian and he was totally loyal to Saud. Mosem would do anything to make sure Saud was happy and would try to get anything Saud wanted, and I mean anything.

He was broad-shouldered, big-bellied, his nose was hooked, his mouth large and narrow and had a muscular force about him. He smoked like a chimney and he was also very sly.

Mosem would be my interpreter and I thought he was doing a good job of it until I found out later he changed some of the things I'd said, to make it 'sound' better, he told me. With some people you start off on the wrong foot and you can't get back on balance, you're constantly hopping; I could feel there was already tension between us.

Showtime

Nick and Mosem had arranged the space and paid for the week so all I needed to do was turn up and demonstrate my software.

Ha! I turned up a day before the show was due to open and

a good job too. There was a space, just a space, no tables, no chairs, no signs or computer equipment. No problem, this is Saudi Arabia, says Nick. We'll improvise, they'll love it.

We borrowed a couple of desks and two extension leads. I had a laptop, or more of a luggable as it weighed a ton. Nick borrowed a big screen from work and printed some posters and I had brought brochures and flyers to hand out. In western terms we looked amateurish and I was wondering what I had signed up for. Mosem had a brainwave: curtains, we needed some net curtains and big pots. What the…? Help!

Wow, what a stand. We wrapped some net curtains around the legs of the stand at the front and back and draped a couple across the roof. Placed the pots on the corners and it looked like a boudoir, very enticing, genius.

It was too late to start worrying and if nothing worked we hadn't lost much. I hoped it was enough.

The next day the show opened and there was some bigwig royal guy being shown around before the crowds were allowed in.

'Assalaamu Aleikum,' he said as he passed.

'You have to say wa aleikum Assalaam wa rahmatullah wa barakaatuh to reply,' said Mosem.

'Right!! I'll remember that,' I answered. Fat chance, it will probably take me a year to learn that lot.

He had about twenty people in his entourage, some with gold braid on their robes and some with guns hidden under theirs. He stopped at every stand and asked one of his team what we were selling; he looked very disinterested and classed it as a chore he could do without. I should have taken more notice of him as he would become a big part of my life in Saudi at a later date.

Once he was out of the way the main doors were opened and all hell broke loose. People were fascinated with the merchandise but had no idea what most of it was. Everyone wanted a new toy but unless they were there on business it was a waste of time. People just looking around wondering why what was going on. It was a computer show and ninety percent of the population didn't own a home computer. What the hell do you do with a graphics card? Or what do I need a modem for, what's a mouse? You can't sell anything at the right price, everyone wants a discount. They all barter as if it's an Arabic souk. How much discount can I get?

As soon as people found out what I had to show they moved on. I was asked for my photograph which I thought was flattering until Nick told me why.

'They just want to use it to blackmail you,' he said. 'It's illegal to photograph someone without their consent.'

Lunchtime came and everyone cleared out.

'Come on, might as well go home for a couple of hours, it's siesta time until four,' said Nick.

'What about my laptop?' I said. 'I'm not leaving it here to be nicked.'

'Nobody will touch it, there's no crime here. People get their hands cut off if they are caught,' said Mosem.

'OK, if you're sure,' I said.

***

A couple of days after I got there I called home and spoke to my Dad and he encouraged me to keep at it and he was sure I could get something out of it, but my mum was not so sure.

'You do know Iraq are moving their army towards you, don't you?' she said. 'The Americans are calling it "Operation Vigilant Warrior".'

'Stop worrying,' I told her. 'I'm only here another few days and I've got a return flight booked.' I hadn't even considered there might be another war. Oh well, I wasn't going anywhere; the show must go on as they say.

What a waste of time. I spent a week trying to get some interest but it's hard when you don't speak the lingo. Nick's comment to me during that first phone call was not true; it's not easy to sell to the Arabs.

Mosem was with me the whole week but he isn't a salesman and he didn't know anything about my products. So he took business cards from anyone who had one and we had a draw for a meal out in Al-Khobar. This proved to be a way of at least getting people to stop at our stand. I planned to call some of them after the show finished. Mosem was definitely living up to his name of getting things for you.

So the show was a bit of a disaster. Told you so, said my partners, Ron, Martin and Laurence, in London. I had to report in every other day and it wasn't good news.

I wasn't giving up yet though.

Stay or Go

Nick and Kaitlin were brilliant. I stayed at their villa for the week and they made me feel at home as best they could. Seaview was like an English holiday camp with a pool, tennis courts and a gym but without the social club or entertainment. Each villa had two bedrooms and they gave me their spare bedroom. Their daughter still slept in a cot in their room.

During the week every evening Nick tried to persuade me to stay. He said it was not easy to make a lot of progress after only a week at a small trade show. It was a massive decision for me and I was not convinced. I had a family in England and I missed them. My wife was OK with what I decided and knew I would make it work.

Nick's company were into computer aided design and he knew my software would save them time and money in the long term.

We visited Saud halfway through the week to update him on our progress. He knew Saudi Arabia was a nation of slow, laid back people looking for a bargain who seemed never to be rushed.

So I had a decision to make. Commit to a long stay or go home for good. I had planned a ten day visit and my return flight was pre-arranged.

My Saudi visa entitled me to a three month stay so I could use the time to find out if it was worth staying. I went to Nick's office and he showed me the work they were doing using similar software to mine. He was having problems with suppliers and thought the region needed a professional outfit. He thought a new approach would take a lot of business from his suppliers. They had had it easy for too long and he was willing to put the word around. The office block where he worked had loads of companies on different floors and he took me to a scanning company called Arabscan a few floors down who said they were having similar problems.

After explaining that the best rival I would have was pretty unhelpful and technical support was virtually zero I was convinced. The task in hand was a bit daunting to say the least. To open an office and build a client network, I would need introductions. So stay was the more profitable option but I would need a lot of help. I had a flashback to my childhood, straying outside my comfort zone, exploring a world holding mysteries beyond me.

So I went back to England and explained all this to my family and my partners at the office. It didn't go all that well at first, but they knew when I put my mind to something there was no changing it. I had some time off with the family and arranged another trip.

Not straightforward this time, as the embassy would need all my details to issue me with a work visa to replace my visit one.

Chapter 3

Joint Venture

It's a Matter of Trust

As a limited company registered in the UK we decided to call my new venture a branch office. Saud became our sponsor as well as mine individually, and we called it a joint venture. We would supply me (and Ron now and again), the computers, both hardware and software, and Saud would supply the office, all the furniture, some expense money to get up and running and more importantly a car.

To work in Saudi Arabia is totally different from travelling there on a visit visa. Your sponsor needs to arrange with the Saudi chamber of commerce that the job you're going to do for him is one that can't be filled by a Saudi national. Sponsors have to list the employees they require and the roles they will fill within their company and where these employees are from. Only a certain number can come from each region around the world to make it fairer, for instance, a few each from America, Africa, Australia, Canada, Europe, India, Indonesia, The Philippines or

Scandinavia. So if your quota of Europeans is filled you have to employ from one of the other regions. Also the wage structure depends where they are from. Higher pay for jobs filled with people from the USA and down the scale. Qualifications also affect the status of each employee. As I don't have a degree I can't be employed as a manager or similar role. As Saud wasn't actually employing me I could basically do what the new venture required.

I made an appointment at the Saudi Arabian embassy in London took my passport and thought it was going to be straightforward.

Well, it is if you know what you are doing, and it seems I didn't. Looking back I should have used an agency but I thought I knew best, again I didn't.

You need to queue first to get a form, and then fill it in telling them why on earth you would ever want to go to their country. Take a number and wait to be called and then give them the form back with your passport and a photo of yourself.

'Where's your medical certificate?' asked the desk clerk.

'What! I wasn't told about that,' I replied.

'You need to have a full medical before we can process your visa,' he said. 'Come back when you've got it and we'll finish your visa request.'

I called Martin at the office and asked him if he could organise a medical for me. I knew I could go to my doctor but I thought he would know of a quicker way. He booked me into a clinic in Harley Street for the following day. Harley Street? Jesus, that's a bit posh; the only doctors I'd been to before was on Shrublands estate in Croydon. When I got there I explained I needed it for a Saudi Arabian visa. The receptionist knew what I needed and explained it was a requirement that I have an HIV test as well. Blimey, I'd no idea that would be needed; it was a bit scary. So after waiting half an hour or so thinking the worst I met the doctor, who was really nice, and I had my medical. I had to wait a bit after but it was worth it because they gave me all the results before I left and thankfully I was fit and well in all areas. God knows how much that cost.

I thought I'd take my two sons with me the next day for the trip in London. So I went back the following day and presented my new medical certificate and thought that was that but no, they keep your passport and tell you to come back the following day between 12 and 2pm. I thought that was a bit dodgy leaving my passport there, but it was take it or leave it. They kept us waiting so long we didn't have much of a day out. This was becoming a week's worth of travelling to London.

OK, so I got my visa and started to arrange the travel. I bought a one way ticket and not for one minute did I think I wouldn't be coming back. I didn't know about the exit visa yet.

Martin organised a small shipment of computers complete with large screens to be sent to Saud's office.

When I arrived back in Saudi Nick met me by himself this time, but we still managed to avoid the passport control queues. We went straight to Seaview for me to rest for a bit.

The following day I went with Mosem to the chamber of commerce in Dammam to get my iqama (residency permit). This was to be to be carried at all times. What I didn't know was it is common practice in Saudi Arabia for your sponsor to hold onto your passport, under the labour law guidelines, whilst you retain your iqama for day to day purposes.

You cannot leave the country without an exit visa being granted, at a cost, and that's only if your sponsor allows you to leave. There are heavy fines, sometimes accompanied with prison sentences if you overstay your visa or do not hold the correct type of visa. It started to dawn on me what I was getting into when I exchanged my passport for my iqama. I thought as this was a business arrangement, Saud would trust me and I would be allowed to come and go as I pleased. How wrong could I be?

It usually takes about three months to process a new iqama but as Saud knows just about everyone, mine would be ready in a week.

In the time it took me to get organised at home Saud and Mosem had sorted out an office. It was a walled villa not far from Prince Turki Street, or the Corniche, as it was called in Al-Khobar. It was out of town and when I saw it I thought it looked like a residential place, but when I went inside they had furnished it with all I would need. It had a reception area with three offices plus a small kitchen and toilet. Thankfully there was air conditioning. It was very different from the 'London' office; well, not quite London, as it was Raynes Park near Wimbledon in south London, but as far as Saud and Mosem were concerned it was my 'London office' and I was keeping it that way.

I also had an assistant. He – I was told it had to be a man because of Saudi employment rules – was called Hesham and like Mosem was also Egyptian. I'm already thinking the Egyptian mafia.

At the rear of the offices Mosem had arranged for some accommodation for Hesham. Running along the back wall of the villa and the outside wall was a tin roof and beneath this a makeshift room had been made for my assistant. I assume it had been the maid's quarters in the past. It had a bed and the outside toilet had been made into a small shower room. It would be like living inside a furnace. Hesham said he was used to this type of place and told me not to worry about him.

I had to wait for the shipment to arrive from London before I could get fully up and running.

I thought I'd better start learning the Hindi numbering system. It's a bit funny for me to explain so here goes. A zero is a dot. A one is a one. A two is a backward seven. A three is a backward seven with a wobbly top. A four is a backward three. A five is naught. A six is seven. A seven is a V. An eight is an upside down V. A nine is a nine.

So that makes me 'E1' years old. Well, it sort of looks like that. No rush!

Settling in

While the paperwork was finalised at the chamber of commerce I had to book into the Park Inn hotel (now the Radisson) in downtown Al-Khobar. It was almost a 2 star when I stayed there. I couldn't use the new office yet so I used a small room in Saud's office. I visited Nick's company to see the kind of equipment they were using. It was mostly expensive American gear, so I thought I might have an option for him if he needed.

I needed a car so Saud asked Mosem to find me a nice little run-around. He said it had to be white due to the temperature and a Toyota due to the price. Nice, I thought, I'd seen a great little green and white Toyota Rav4 I liked the look of.

Next, I needed a Saudi driving licence. Simple, I thought, I've been driving over twenty years. Ha! Not so easy, the tests are not like in England.

No problem. Saud asked another of his old school mates, none other than the chief of police, to fast track me. So Mosem drove me to police headquarters and I have some afternoon tea and a nice chat with the police chief. He's OK with the licence but I must have an eye test first in case I'm blind and he's not signing the papers till I'm checked out. The test is not a simple 'can you read that number plate', no, a full blown eye test and the report to prove it. Still, I had his business card and if ever I needed help I could call him, and call him I would. Saud was indeed a very good guy to know. I started a collection of business cards. I like little accumulations of this and that to stir memories.

The driving test is another thing entirely. They hold them in a test centre, they daren't let you out on the roads yet, it's like an army barracks, and you have to drive around an obstacle course, including reversing into a small space and parking against a wall between rows of parked cars. This was nearly impossible for me as the car was left hand drive, which was new to me. I'd driven on the right before but never been tested. Car rental companies usually trust your English licence. My new police chief mate explained it was all to do with reversing. You see, most drivers arrive in this country from India and have never reversed a car in their life before. If you pass the reversing test you pass the complete test. Which I did, and only because my new mate organised for me to do it on my own and with him supervising it. Unheard of before, the chief of police officiating a driving test for an expat. The other guys being tested were tested in batches of around six men all trying to pass simultaneously. It was like banger racing at Wimbledon.

So I got a new green Saudi driving license with squiggly writing that I couldn't understand and a brand new white 'Toyota Cressida' estate car with red leather seats and, thank god, the most important item, air conditioning. Thanks, Mosem.

I was beginning to enjoy this. Not for long though. You can't live in a hotel forever. Although I wish I'd stayed there.

Filling the car with petrol was an eye opener as well because you could fill it for a fiver. The oil price was so high and the petrol cost very low.

When it came to driving, though, it was a nightmare. At every traffic light cars were in the wrong lane, especially me. The inside lane allowed turning at traffic lights but there was always someone wanting to go straight ahead so he ended up turning across the four lanes to his left, completely in front of the cars waiting to go ahead. Horns were blasting continuously. All of the Indian drivers used to sound their horn just as the lights turned green it was very annoying. Once I was in a long queue and after a couple of lights changed and I was still waiting I got out and walked back to the car behind to ask him to stop honking every time the light changed. He looked so scared and obviously thought I was going to hit him. He cowered in his seat and accused me of racism because he was coloured. Well, that nearly got him a black eye or two. I'm not interested where you come from or your religion, if I think you're wrong I'll let you know.

When the computers arrived I called Ron and he came out to help get things going. We also had Mosem to kickstart our little venture. This was beginning to cost us a bit in flights for Ron, and the London office were looking for some money in return for their investment.

No Palace in Al-Khobar

When you need somewhere to live as cheaply as possible, Mosem is your man. Basically if you want anything cheap ask Mosem. As I said before, he was there to get Saud anything he wanted, and this passed to me. The difference between us is Mosem is from Egypt and I'm from England and what he thinks is ideal to live in I think is a hovel. I don't think I'm a snob as such but a one bedroom flat in downtown Al-Khobar is a hovel. It was my own fault, I should have asked for a bit more upmarket and not cheap; still, there's a limit even to my standards.

Anyway beggars can't be choosers and I didn't have a lot of choice. The entrance hallway was dark and dingy, lacking in any form of decoration, not much lighting, and a receptionist kiosk. There were three floors, no lift and my place was on the second. As I entered the apartment, dust motes danced in slow-motion as the sunlight streamed through the small bared windows. Ron, god bless him, was very helpful; he went out and bought a load of cleaning gear. While he was out I looked at the bars on the windows and thought it was like being locked in. Still, it was better than nothing so when he got back we set to work scrubbing the place. The kitchen would have been closed down if it were a restaurant, even the cockroaches had nasty coughs. The lounge, or sitting room as they called it, was drab and the furniture was very low without legs or feet and it was as if you were sitting on the floor. There was a small table and two hard backed chairs. I had no television so I planned to buy a radio/cassette and CD player. There were plenty of pirate music shops on every corner so easy to get most of the latest albums.

I took a three month lease and decided to buy bottled water and eat out as much as I could. So I ate out and it was an experience, I discovered Taco Bell, Wendy's, Pizza Hut, Thai, Indian and Lebanese food. I was used to fish and chips and macaroni cheese.

My favourite was a small Mediterranean place not far from the office called Baba Habas, where I spent most of my lunchtimes for grilled chicken or shish kebabs. Nick took me to an Indian café which sold a traditional curry in metal trays for a pound. There were about fifty people sitting at Formica tables. No spare tables, so we had to join a couple on a table for four. They were surprised when I asked for a spoon and fork as they all eat with their hands, or their right hand anyway. They sold a book of thirty tickets to last a month, not a bad deal, a meal a day for a pound.

Without air conditioning my life would have been absolute hell, and there was an old one by the window so I shut the window and fiddled with the big unit until I had it adjusted to send a vague panting of warm air into the room, accompanied by such a grinding and rattling and droning that all sounds of the outside world were gone.

***

Next was a bank account and after asking around I open one with the Saudi British Bank. It was affiliated with the Midland Bank in the UK so my wife could get some money at home without any transfer fees. I arranged for two debit cards and sent one home with Ron, who passed it on to my wife. It's not easy running two homes and I still had a mortgage and had to pay for my family at home while keeping myself as well. So I had to split my pay with the majority going home. It was different for Nick and Kaitlin as they didn't have any property in England to pay for, and Kaitlin was a hairdresser so she was able to run a small business from their villa as well.

Traditionally, Al-Khobar is a city of shopkeepers and merchants, and the city today has many modern malls and boulevards with shops run by international franchises and restaurants.

There are many supermarkets which carry the full range (with the obvious exceptions) of goods available in western supermarkets. Shopping malls are full of familiar brand names.

A wide range of drugs are available without prescription. One such shopping centre in town was called The Shula. It was on three floors and you could buy most things you needed to live. I bought cleaning products, new bedding, pots, pans, crockery and cutlery. I was not planning on getting ill any time soon. I'd already been bitten on my ankle by a mosquito and needed antiseptic cream. So I also bought a net to cover the bed. I tried to make it as comfortable as possible. While shopping I noticed that all the shop workers were Indian or Pakistani men. Even the women's clothes shops had male shop assistants. It seemed weird to be served totally by men. Some shopping malls actively discourage single men from entering at certain times or on specific days. Some shops are designated family only, meaning that men cannot enter alone. Changing facilities are limited, with virtually no changing rooms for women. Many shops and restaurants are segregated into singles (male) and family sections. Queues are often two lines separated by a barrier to discourage mixing. Single men should not be in the family section if they are not with their families at the time. Regulations exist governing what separate facilities / entrances have to be available for females. Even in family sections, abayas remain essential and while some women will use it to cover everything, for others it has become another opportunity to exhibit style and fashion. When I came out there was a man hanging around the doorway. He opened his coat and had about twenty watches hanging inside. 'Wanna buy a watch?' he asked me in a quiet voice. No thanks.

I like to explore a city when I'm visiting but this was maddening as I couldn't go to some places because I was single and male. There was a small zoo in the middle of Al-Khobar but I wasn't allowed in because there were women and children in there. No point being a children's entertainer here, you'd never get any work.

There's a couple of things I liked about the place though; one was the price of petrol and the other was that it was inundated with dates, one of my favourite fruits.

Chapter 4

New Boys

Hesham

Hesham was from Hurghada in Egypt and his beaming smile was infectious, he was so eager to please. He was going to be busy as he would act as receptionist, secretary, accountant, gopher and dogsbody. He didn't seem to mind though and couldn't do enough for me. Having left home and travelled to this small office, he was happy to be working and earning. He told me he needed to send some of his money home to his parents as this was expected of all Egyptians.

A couple of days after we got settled and Ron had left, Hesham invited me to lunch. I was completely flustered and worried that he fancied me. Anyway he asked me to come to his place at one o'clock and he would prepare lunch for us. Considering he lived in the shack attached to the office, I couldn't possibly be late and I was thinking it had to be a take-away. Well, I was completely blown away as he had come up with chicken and Mediterranean salad with hummus, dips and pitta bread. How on earth he had done this without any cooking facilities was astounding. I asked him who taught him to cook and he said it's his mum. Wow, my mum only taught me how to boil an egg. He did all this with a camping stove and his own skill.

He was not only a great cook but also a great host. He had laid a 'table' on a box with cushions on the floor for seats. A couple of his friends arrived and we shared his food for the best part of two hours. We talked about our different lives. We were both fascinated about each other's culture. After lunch he wouldn't let me clear up and was apologising for taking such a long lunch. Also, he didn't fancy me.

Buddy

Buddy came from Indonesia and he was my driver. Saud had given us a Pontiac Bonneville and it was Buddy's pride and joy. He was always cleaning it and it was spotless like new. Until I knew my way around, any long drives would be Buddy driving. So I had a bit of luxury for a while.

He had been in Saudi for about three years and had a wife and son living in Bandung, near Jakarta. Saud thought if I was going on any long journeys into the desert to visit a company, I should have a driver who is familiar with the area. Buddy was ideal because he knew every road ever built in the Eastern province. I didn't think he would be very good as a bodyguard though as he was only five foot four tall and weighed about a hundred and thirty pounds. In fact, he had a black belt in Aikido and was always there when I wanted him and never complained. He missed his family a lot but he couldn't change the life he had. He had a two year contract with Saud and he was sending nearly all his money home every month.

A two year contract means just that. You cannot leave the kingdom until you have worked there for twenty three months and then you get a month off. It seems everyone's a prisoner until you've done your time.

I sat in my apartment one evening thinking about this whole scenario of Saudi Arabia and working there. I can only compare it to a film I'd seen called *No Escape.* Prisoners are sent to an island monitored by the wardens, and helicopters patrol to make sure nobody tries to escape. Saudi Arabia was a bit like that in the sense that once you arrive you can't leave until you've done your time or your sponsor signs a release certificate and pays for an exit visa. Your sponsor paid for a return ticket and expected you to return. If you didn't, you were barred from returning unless you returned the fare money. You could resign if you gave three months' notice but life can be pretty bad if you do. You are in a kind of catch-22 situation unless you can save something.

The other side of the coin is that all expats, as they are called, have a sponsor so everyone has a contract therefore everyone has a job and a place to live. No sponsor, no contract, no job, not allowed into Saudi. Sponsors could apply for a three months' visit visa and convert it to a full visa during this time.

I thought I was alright though because I hadn't signed a work contract. Ha!

Ben

We had a visitor one day who introduced himself saying he'd heard a whisper that a new guy was in town. I find Americans are pretty resourceful and in my opinion most are terrific salesmen. Ben was one such American who conducted ninety percent of his business from his car, which was a very nice new Jeep Cherokee; a bit of car envy coming in there. He was in the same business as me albeit a similar and rival software. How he found us I have no idea, but as I said he was resourceful. He was very interested in becoming a dealer for our software and wanted a percentage of any sales he made. I'm always very sceptical of hustlers and that's how he came across. I was blinkered to the opportunity that he offered and must say I regretted it later. He had been in Saudi for five years and knew just about every company that needed our products. I didn't know that at first but I should have given him a chance. I know that now, though. He had done what I proposed to do and knew the ropes. I should have learnt from him but my nature is to be wary until he'd proved himself.

Ben was a nice guy and just wanted to help both me and him. He used to be an offshore underwater welder, which meant he was a terrific diver and a bit of an explorer. He'd built a successful business from scratch all by himself. He employed a few technicians to demonstrate for him but basically he was his own boss and lived alone so he was looking for social company.

Ron arrived for one of his monthly visits and I introduced him to Ben. During an afternoon meeting Ben invited us to dinner at one of his favourite haunts. It was a Malaysian restaurant near Dhahran, a bit secluded and quiet. The staff were really friendly and the food was wonderful. Ben explained to Ron what he proposed and Ron loved the idea. Ron knew I was a terrible salesman and thought Ben was just what we needed. I still needed to believe he wasn't going to take over our business. Ron explained to me later that Ben had so many clients and we had a handful so he didn't need to. All of our clients were the same as his anyway.

Just to prove me wrong, Ben organised a demonstration of my software to one of his best clients and I had to do the demo. If it was a success and we got a sale then we would negotiate a commission after. So a couple of days later he took us to the company for a mid-morning appointment. It was in town so we didn't have far to go. The demo went well and we left Ben to finalise the sale. That afternoon Ben came by and gave us the good news that he had received a positive response and they wanted an official quotation.

That was the start of a great partnership and friendship. Ben would regularly arrive at the door and tell me to get my coat and we'd head off for the day to a client or two.

'No point staying in the office,' he'd say. 'You have to get out there and be seen. Even if they send you away each time, they remember you.'

How right he was. He was so blasé about it one day we turned up out of the blue at Sabic in the industrial city of Al Jubail and walked straight to the canteen for lunch. We joined the queue and were served even though we didn't work there. He'd see people there and they'd ask him how he was and who he'd come to see. He'd make something up and they would ask him to come and see them later. He was always into something.

Where's Hesham

It was the beginning of a new week and I was raring to go, so it was a big surprise when I arrived at my usual time expecting to find Hesham at his desk waiting for me. He wasn't there and gave no answer to my call so I looked for him out the back of the office in his living accommodation. It was deserted. In fact he had deserted us, his personal possessions were gone as well so I knew he'd cleared out. I liked him and wanted to find him but I'd no way of locating him. He hadn't said anything to me about wanting to leave or about being unhappy. It was quite sad because he was in big trouble now, as you cannot change your job or transfer your sponsorship without the agreement of the current sponsor. Saud would not grant a transfer of sponsorship or exit visa to Hesham until his contract was completed. If he'd talked to me about it I could have helped him out. Too late now. Mosem went up the wall and I knew if he caught him he would have him arrested. That's after Mosem had punished him first. I wouldn't like to get on the wrong side of him in a fight.

Still, I needed a replacement and Mosem had to find me one. Oh boy, he found one alright.

Mohammed

Saud asked Mosem to find the perfect replacement. Mosem thought all Egyptians were the best workers so he went back to his contacts for our new guy. Well, he found Mohammed. Poor old Mohammed, he arrived by coach all the way from Cairo via Jordan, a 2400-kilometre journey that took a couple of days. He was shattered when he got to me and all he wanted was a shower and a bed. He had a travel bag with a few clothes and personal possessions, nothing much to show for himself. Mosem wanted him to start immediately but I persuaded him to allow the poor guy at least a day off to recuperate. When Mohammed saw his new home he didn't believe it. He thought he was getting an apartment or at least a room in someone's house. Still, he was so tired he just accepted it and went to get some sleep.

When I arrived the next day he was wide awake and couldn't wait to get started. As soon as I walked in he welcomed me to the office as if it was my first day. He had made some tea for me and brought it to my room on a tray with a glass of water. I thought, it's not my birthday, what's going on here? He certainly wanted to make an impression and he was starting quite well.

How little did I know.

Chapter 5

Finding My Feet

Neil and Simon

Even though the majority of alcohol available in Saudi Arabia is of the homebrew variety, there is also a small supply of properly distilled spirits smuggled into the kingdom.

Nick had been introduced to two guys after the party where he met Saud. They were Neil and Simon who worked for British Aerospace. They lived on Oasis Gardens compound, which is about the most prestigious compound you could get. If you didn't work for Aramco and live on their private compound then you would want Oasis Gardens, if you could afford it; sadly it was too expensive for me.

As there are no legal bars in Saudi where alcohol can be bought, they had converted their villa into a bar. That's why the compounds have barred wire round them to keep the religious police out. Expats or foreigners who drink alcohol in their compound tend to be ignored by the Saudi police. The thing about compounds is that you can't just enter when you want, you have to be invited in. There is an entry hut with guards positioned behind glass windows. There is an entry phone and you need to call the guards and tell them who you were visiting. Most times it has been pre-arranged and the guard has a list with your name on it. If not, he will call the person you are visiting and you can speak to them. The guard will let you in if you've been approved. In Neil and Simon's case they had to restrict the visits to a small crowd or they would be shut down. They also had a camera on their door to see who wanted to visit.

They used to buy home brewed beer and siddiqi from neighbours and charge a small profit. Siddiqi can become many drinks, some like it with tonic water, and some like it with Coke or bitter lemon. These become gin and tonic or rum and Coke. Neil liked to add Jack Daniels wood chips to the bottle and let it mature, so this became brown sid. OK with ginger ale.

As I left to go home one night, I saw a man lying flat out in the street literally on the corner, but sufficiently far away not to tell where he'd been. It was a good thing as long as it wasn't abused. So we made sure we didn't.

Solitude is merciless so I became a frequent visitor to Neil and Simon's bar during those depressing days when I was stuck for entertainment in the evenings. If you feel like a prisoner in a country with no escape, you need some form of outlet.

Bargaining

Nick was my first customer. He needed some computer screens for his office and thought I needed to get going, so suggested they buy from us. He already knew the type he wanted and asked his buying department to place an order with me. He didn't tell me so when I received the call it was a pleasant surprise.

I'd set up our email system and had made templates for all our products so it should have been easy to deal with any purchase order. What I wasn't ready for was the buyer to call and ask for a knock-down price. In England we had set prices and didn't offer a discount unless we bundled software and hardware in a special deal.

'Hi Mr. Dennis, my name is Yousef. I have your prices and I need you to drop the price a bit,' he said.

'Yousef, that's not possible, there's no discount on this particular item,' I replied.

'Mr. Dennis, look it's a problem for me, I can't buy at that price, they are too expensive,' he said.

'It's the going rate, Yousef, exactly how many do you need?' I asked.

'We need three,' he replied. 'Look, this is Saudi, you have to bargain here.'

'I don't know about that, that's OK in the market or the souk but this is office equipment,' I replied.

'Mr. Dennis, maybe one item but three, it's the same everywhere, we are a nation of bargainers,' he said. 'Please have a think and I will call you back tomorrow.'

I had to think of a way round this but I knew I'd have to give in and lower my initial price.

I called Nick. 'Your buyer is trying to get me to lower my price to save you some money.'

'Oh yes, I forgot to warn you about that.'

'Well, I wasn't prepared for it and it threw me a bit, I need to think of a way round it.'

'It's a lot to do with face. He has to be seen to bargain the price down so he looks good to his superiors and gets a good bonus,' he said.

'Well, it's not good for my profit margin.'

I met him after work and we talked about a strategy for bargaining in the future. I slept on it, rather badly. It's just a sale for Christ's sake, nothing to lose sleep about. It was personal though, it was Nick and he was doing me a favour. When I woke I had decided to give a little for the sale to go through. Also he may want more later, then there was Saud to consider – he had to see it was all worth it. So reporting our first sale was important to us all.

Nick went in the following day and asked about his new screens. The buyer told him he was working on a deal and would deliver them ASAP. The problem Nick had was he couldn't tell him he knew me, as it would be seen as a conflict and they would go elsewhere. He told him he had three guys waiting downstairs unable to work because they needed screens and the buyer was costing the company money every minute his men couldn't produce any work. So he had better get on with it. Nick hoped this would prompt him to get the deal done quickly.

I got the call mid-morning but I'd already decided to give him a better price. I wanted to learn from this so I bargained.

'Hello, Mr. Dennis, have you decided on a new price for me,' he asked.

'I'd like to know how much you think they are worth,' I replied.

'Oh, I'd like you to drop at least twenty percent,' he said.

'That's too much, how about five percent?' I prompted.

'Come on, you can do better than that. How about fifteen.'

'I can't drop lower than seven,' I said.

'OK, let's go with ten,' he said.

I needed the last word.

'Fine, you can have eight and that's final,' I said.

'Well done Mr. Dennis, I knew you had some leeway and now we have a deal, I'm happy with that,' he said.

At last. I'd lost a bit but I'd made a sale and learnt the hard way to put all prices up before starting the bargaining. This wasn't going to be plain sailing.

Crash

In earlier days, Al-Khobar was a small port on the Persian Gulf coast, a fishing village inhabited mainly by Al Dossary tribe members. With the discovery of oil in the 1930s, it was transformed into a commercial and shopping centre and an industrial port. As a result, Al-Khobar has transformed and extended its water front along the Arabian Gulf into a corniche with parks, restaurants and family beaches.

It is laid out like a grid and the road layout is all one way streets, north up, south down, east right, west left, no roundabouts, straight roads. I must admit it was becoming a lonely life so I usually went to the office every day just for something to do. On this particular Friday – by the way, the weekend is Thursday and Friday in the Arab world – it was a nice sunny day, not a lot about so I was leisurely driving along King Khalid Road. I'd been browsing the shops and was on my way to the office when a car came flying out of a side road and hit the back wing of my car. I spun a few times and ended up all wrong facing the oncoming traffic. 'Inshallah' it was only a Friday or I'd be brown bread. I managed to stop the car spinning and reverse into the curb. The other driver was in the middle of the main road, he had his family with him and they were all still in the car crying. He was out and screaming at me.

As far as I was concerned, I was in the right, and he had pulled out of side turning and hit me. I had the dents to prove it; my back wing was severely damaged. Well, what I didn't know was the Saudi rules about car accidents. You have to stay where you are and not move until the police arrive, however long it takes. Me, I just wanted to get out of people's way and not cause any more damage. Their drivers are a nightmare as it is.

He was accusing me of causing the accident by the fact that I shouldn't have been there in the first place. It's like a being in the wrong place at the wrong time scenario. The reason you mustn't move the vehicles is so the police can ascertain whose fault it is. Normally they can see by where the cars are positioned who's at fault. I had moved my car but because the other driver knew he was liable he drove away.

Where is Mosem when you need him? I had to find a phone and saw a pharmacy close by so I ran there and asked for help. He came when I called and ran the riot act with me. Now I had a problem, as the other driver was gone and I couldn't prove whose fault it was. He knew he was at fault and acted quickly when he saw a stupid Englishman.

'If you don't get a police report you can't get the car repaired on insurance,' Mosem explained.

There was no way out of this, and Saud would get the bill for repair even though I'd been the innocent party.

'It's not only that,' he said. 'Everywhere you go the police will ask how that happened.'

So I had to borrow Buddy's pride and joy until we could get my car repaired. Nevertheless Saud called my chief of police mate and he smoothed it over for me.

Even though I was used to driving a left hand drive car, the Pontiac had an automatic gearbox with the gear change behind the steering wheel, so it took me a few goes to get used to it. I felt a bit special driving it and wanted to keep driving it. Buddy could have my car if it ever got repaired.

I went to Ben's apartment and he offered me a much needed beer, a bottle of Grolsch lager no less, and boy was it strong.

How? Well, there are supermarkets in Saudi just like in England or the USA, and they offer the same variety of food and drink. The only difference is the drink has no alcohol in it. Every type of beer or wine but the alcohol has been removed. So you can go down the beer isle and buy all you favourites. Grolsch bottles have resealable tops so are brilliant for home brew. Ben would buy a trolley load of the stuff and take it home and empty it into a water butt, then add some yeast and sugar then wait a while until it came to life. Then put it back in the bottles and it would be like rocket fuel, very dangerous if you drank too much. He said if you want home brew, start with something that's almost there, not like the stuff some guys made from scratch. He was on about siddiqi, the most popular home brew spirit. It is often shortened to sid. It varies in strength but is a lot stronger than standard spirits available in the west. Sid can be as strong as 90% alcohol, and it often also contains impurities. It needed to be cut 60/40 with water or could be a killer. I was told of a book called 'The Blue Flame' explaining how to make it, but I never got a copy.

***

Living in town was getting to me. I wanted to be closer to the new friends I'd made. When I came to move I found out another difference from England, the calendar. Saudi dates are calculated in accordance with the Hijri Islamic calendar. It is a lunar calendar consisting of 12 months in a year of 354 or 355 days. So after my rental agreement was up, I tried to leave but the landlord wanted another three days' rent. It all depends which day of the month you move in. I was packed up and ready to go but even though but I showed him the contract which stated the moving in date and it was exactly three months before, I still needed to pay. This is 1995 and they were in 1415. Still, I couldn't wait to get out of there so I paid.

I moved to an apartment on Seaview compound. It was a small studio flat and suited me down to the ground. It was much cleaner then the last place and the compound was gated and felt safer, like a small village. There were tennis courts and Nick challenged me to a match a few times a week. He always won and told everyone he thrashed me but neglected to tell anyone every game went to deuce. No killer instinct, that's my trouble, according to Nick. He is thirteen years younger than me by the way, with a massive killer instinct. Also, I wasn't going to kill myself as I had no health care arranged yet.

There wasn't any health care in Saudi Arabia so I needed to arrange medical insurance. Nick introduced me to his close friend Keith. He sold insurance and health policies to expats in the kingdom. He lived in Bahrain and was a regular visitor to Saudi. He arranged for insurance to transport me home if I ever needed it. Also, as I couldn't contribute to my English pension fund while I was working abroad, he opened a bank account for me that would facilitate an offshore pension. I was very grateful as I hadn't a clue how to arrange these things by myself. People like Keith were a must for all expats who required insurance abroad. His sales technique was reassuring; so much so we became friends, and he regularly visited me for a morning cup of tea or coffee. He would bring donuts or croissants and we'd chat about life in general. I fancied a trip to Bahrain and he was always offering me a place to stay if ever I got there.

What Did It Say?

I had a call from my wife about my American Express card bill. She said it was rather a lot last month which surprised her. My mail was still being sent to my home in England and she had to pay all the bills while I was away and coped very well usually, but this had thrown her accounts out a lot. I asked her to read out the statement and there were a couple of flights showing that I hadn't booked. She said they were from the booking agency I used for my flights. When I called them about it, they said it was down to me, but I explained I where I was and couldn't have taken those flights. They apologised and said they would look into it for me. It turned out the operator who booked my flight had also booked the next two flights for his mates using my credit card details. He probably thought I would be away a while and not check my statement for a few months, but thanks to my missus he got caught. I got a full refund and a written apology but it goes to show you need to check them regularly.

***

Ron came to visit us every few months and in March and we had been doing OK, but he thought we needed a jump start. So he tried to push us to new heights. Firstly we needed to get some money in from sales and he wanted to see the invoice book. Mohammed had been keeping them and Ron asked to see them. It was probably my fault because I been too busy out on sales to check Mohammed's book keeping, but he was meant to be qualified in accounting. The folder containing the invoices was not in order and there was no record if we had received the money on each invoice. So Ron got hold of the book and tried to ascertain if we were owed much. He called Mohammed and asked him if each invoice had been paid.

'I'm not sure, Mr. Ron,' said Mohammed.

'Surely you know if we've received the money,' answered Ron.

'Sorry Mr. Ron, I'll have to check the bank statement,' said Mohammed.

'The bank statements are sometimes a month behind the dates you paid the funds in,' said Ron. Mohammed was lost for words; he couldn't see the problem. People would pay, they just took their time sometimes. Nobody pushed too hard in Saudi. Well, Ron was having none of it and decided to show Mohammed how he should be running the accounts.

He said to Mohammed, 'I bet that plant in the corner of the office knows as much as you do about this invoice.' Then he turned to the plant and asked it, 'Has this invoice been paid?'

No answer. Mohammed was looking at Ron with a vacant expression of a deer watching an oncoming vehicle.

'There,' said Ron. 'That plant knows the same as you, Mohammed.'

'What did it say?' asked Mohammed.

'Nothing,' said Ron. 'Absolutely nothing.'

I could see Ron's stress level rising so I said, 'Ron, let's go out. I think I can solve this.'

We went to the Shula shopping centre and I bought him a coffee and we also bought a stamp and ink pad. When we got back Ron proceeded to show Mohammed how they worked.

Ron called him into my office.

'Mohammed, we've bought something to help you keep track of the invoices. This is a paid stamp and this is an ink pad,' he said. 'It has the date on it which you can change to today and stamp each invoice when you receive the cheque, that way any that are not stamped you will know they haven't been paid yet.'

'Wow,' said Mohammed, 'that is amazing, then what?'

'Then we have to call them and ask for the payment,' said Ron. 'You have to tell Mr. Dennis they have not paid and he will chase them up.'

'But what if they still don't pay?' he said.

'That is Mr. Dennis' problem, not yours,' said Ron.

'So I still don't have any problems, they pay when they want,' said Mohammed.

'But Mr. Dennis might be able to get the money quicker and it's good for our bank balance,' said Ron.

'Good luck with that then,' Mohammed said, giggling.

Anyway we carried on in and out of the office, meeting a few companies, trying our best to show our stuff and after a few days we came back to the office in the afternoon and heard a *thump thump thump* noise coming from Mohammed's main reception area.

'What's going on and what's that noise, Mohammed?' I asked.

'I'm practising,' he said.

'What with?' I asked.

'I'm making sure I've got this stamping thing right,' he said.

I looked at the paper on his desk and it was covered in date stamps, left, right, upside down, horizontal, vertical, on the back of the sheet, everywhere and each with a different date.

I went to check the invoice book and the stamps were upside down or on the back of the page.

'That's Mohammed for you,' I said.

My first Big Sale

As I was new to the area the main representative for my main product came to see me. He introduced himself as Omar from Somalia and he was the Middle East representative. He was really tall and had ebony coloured skin and ivory coloured teeth with a bald head. He looked like a marathon runner he was so thin; very smartly dressed, though, in a business suit and white linen shirt. He worked for a massive worldwide company and I couldn't believe I'd just met their main man in Saudi. He promised me all the support I needed and I was to call him anytime. I would definitely be needing his help sooner rather than later.

My first big sale was to a small design office with a dozen engineers. The company had been going for about ten years and was run by two English men, Duncan and Stewart. The sale included a network with a dozen computers and printing facilities. It was quite a big job for me on my own so I had to phase it over four visits and work around them for downtime. It went OK and we were all pleased with the outcome. Duncan and Stewart lived together and were very good friends. They actually became good friends of mine and advised me many times about Saudi life and business. I learnt a lot about partnership contracts and employment laws from them. They asked me if I could do some of the work over a weekend so as not to disrupt their workflow too much. After the first weekend and during the installation they came in looking a bit annoyed and I thought it was my work that had caused a problem. They explained that they had been burgled on the Thursday night and most of their clothes and personal things had been taken. I told them to report it to the police. Can't, said Duncan, we have a still in our garage full of siddiqi and also the police would want to interview everyone we have contact with. Close us down and fingerprint everyone in the office. I could call the chief of police but I certainly didn't want my details in the police files, and I'd seen Stewart's stripy jackets and I thought they had been burgled to order; there's another problem with Saudi law.

To celebrate my biggest sale to date I called Nick and suggested we go to Neil's for a drink. We arrived at Neil's place to hear the latest gossip. There was always plenty of news about the local expatriates. Some bloke called Sean had come onshore from one of the oil rigs and been searched at customs. The stupid guy only had dope on him. Well, they'd locked him up and threw away the key. Neil said he'd be deported and everyone had to keep their head down for a few weeks.

I was more interested in finding out about a villa that had blown up on Dossary compound at the weekend. It had been a massive explosion that I'd heard from my place in Seaview, so I asked Simon about it. He said the guy had a still in the back room and he'd gone to Bahrain for the weekend when it had exploded and taken the villa with it. The religious police were itching to get onto the compound to investigate and search for more but the local bobbies had blocked it. Nasty bunch, those religious boys. Thank god for compounds, I keep saying lately.

Where's The Bank?

I usually paid the cheques into the bank but during one of Ron's visits I had an appointment and I wanted to get a particular couple of cheques paid in, so I asked Ron to pay them in for us. The bank was downtown and Ron didn't know the ropes yet, so I asked Mohammed to go with him. Ron had my car and I went out with Buddy. Mohammed was really excited to be getting a trip out of the office, especially with Ron, who I think he secretly adored. Ron told me all this later that evening. Ron drove and Mohammed had the cheques and paying in books. They were driving down Alnuman Ibn Harithah Street and on to King Khalid Road, where the bank is. Ron always likes to talk and he was telling Mohammed something about his home in England so they continued on almost into Dammam.

'Where is the bank?' asked Ron.

'Back there in King Khalid Road,' replied Mohammed.

'What?! Why didn't you tell me to stop?' said Ron.

'Your story was so fascinating and I was enjoying it so much I didn't want to interrupt you,' he replied.

Well, you can imagine by now Ron's pulling his hair out, not that he had much to start with mind you. They turned around, came back and just managed to get there before it was too late for paying in. I laughed and laughed after work when Ron told me about it; Ron was nearly bald by then.

'He's just incompetent. Trust me, it's not contagious,' I said.

Chapter 6

Spring

Up to Khafji

Ben gave me a tip that an oil company in Khafji needed some computer equipment. He said that the Arabian Consulting Engineering Company wanted some new computers. So I arranged a demonstration of a new style PC and large screen.

Khafji is a main industrial city very close to the border with Kuwait that used to be in the Saudi-Kuwait neutral zone. It was occupied by the Iraqi forces during the Gulf War. Saudi forces aided by United States Marines victoriously engaged in the Battle of Khafji during Operation Desert Storm to free it from the Iraqis.

It's a 200 mile (320km) drive from Al-Khobar to Khafji. That's at least two and half to three hours up the coast, and Ben advised me not to go on my own. Thank god he did. I arranged it for one of Ron's trips and when he arrived and I told him about it, he wanted to go straight away.

On the day of the demo we set off early to avoid too much

heat. The drive out from Al-Khobar was pleasant enough, but as we left the main city I suggested we take the Al Jubail road as Ron hadn't been there yet. It's not a very busy road but like all Saudi roads it's very straight and surrounded by desert, it's very monotonous.

I always felt a flutter of nerves which was a variant of my performance anxiety, so as Ron drove I sat with the air conditioning blasting on my face, barely denting the perspiration that was a by-product of my preparation for the demo. We drove through a land of rock and scrub, sand and brush, lizards and the sand-wink of un-rusted soda cans. The area we were travelling through is on the Tropic of Cancer and the temperature was beginning to soar although it would get hotter in a few weeks.

Ron's eyes nearly popped out as we approached Jubail. The landscape was covered with petrochemical companies servicing the oil and gas industry, water plants and steel plants.

'If we can't make a sale here we should give up,' he said.

'I know what you mean but it's not as easy as you imagine,' I replied. 'We'll come back with Ben in a couple of days, he knows everyone.

'Keep going, we're not even half way there yet,' I told him.

So we carried on past the protected area inhabited by tropical fish and marine growth. We kept going and suddenly the road petered out and we were facing sand dunes on all sides. It was a narrow sand and gravel road through a burned land and I could see the contours of the land on either side of us. We climbed into a course jungle of huge tilts of rock, small buttes rising out of sand, and the road found its windy way through this Martian land.

I was thinking we were lost but Ron kept going.

'We're going in the right direction, this road must join a main road somewhere around here,' said Ron.

'Yes, but we're on a road where there is no road,' I said. 'We've long since left anything resembling a road.'

He carries on driving for a good five minutes until we're

almost stuck in sand, then we decide to turn around. At that moment a man with a herd of camels comes out of nowhere and approaches us. In Arabic he said, 'What are you doing here on my property?' Obviously we couldn't understand him so he was pointing and prodding our car and trying to push us away.

'We're heading for Khafji,' said Ron.

'We need to get to Khafji,' he repeated.

'Don't bother,' I said.

If we didn't have a boot full of computer stuff I would have offered to swap our car for a couple of camels.

'Reverse then turn around when you can, we'll have to go back.'

'I'm sure we've just missed the turn off.'

So we went back the way we came for a few miles and noticed a track heading inland. It's better inland than outland so we headed that way. Eventually after another few miles we found the main route 95. Turn right for Khafji. We were so close we'd been travelling parallel to it but a bit closer to the coast. Along the way we saw scud missile towers dotted along the coastline. A reminder of where we were going and the war zone that was only half a decade ago.

We finally arrived in Khafji and it was a border town so the security should be pretty good. It's only 12 miles (33km) from the Kuwaiti border and 80 miles from Kuwait City. Tired and thirsty after our eventful drive, we searched for our destination. Luck would have it it's on the way into town, so just off the main highway.

At reception we explained we had got an appointment with the research and development department chief. We were asked to wait but offered tea and water. Arabic tea is hardly thirst quenching but it's rude to decline. Our contact arrived and we were ushered into a conference room, very posh. We moved our equipment in and set up the demo. The first problem occurred with the plugs and sockets. We had English plugs and they had some weird type I hadn't encountered before, so they weren't prepared for us. Someone managed to find an adapter so at least we could plug our four bar extension in, but it was a bit short. I was feeling like a disaster was happening but Ron was in full flow so I let him talk them round. He ended up showing some super pictures on the big screen while a couple dozed and a few looked absolutely bored out of their skin. They thanked us and said they would let us know, but we knew it was a waste of time.

All that way and we couldn't give the full benefit of what we had brought with us.

It's a massive learning curve just to get one sale. The companies are so far apart, they are not geared for you when you arrive and they are not interested most of the time. As we drove out I suggested checking out the border, so we drove up and had a look at the border post. Two guys were slouching on chairs by a hut looking so bored. We didn't want to bother them so we turned and drove away.

Who is Mr. Dennis?

I used to visit Nick and Kaitlin some evenings after work and one day Nick asked me why I hadn't been returning his calls. I'm bewildered and confused as I've not been receiving any messages to call him.

'What are you on about? I've not had any messages to call you,' I said.

'I've left messages for you at the office to call me,' he said. 'I was beginning to think you were ignoring me.'

'No, I wouldn't do that. I'll ask Mohammed about it,' I said.

'Ben says the same too,' said Nick. 'He's tried to contact you a few times.'

'What? Oh my god, that's terrible. I'll have a go at Mohammed tomorrow when I see him.'

The next day I asked Mohammed why he hadn't been passing my messages on when people called and I wasn't in the office.

'But you haven't had any messages, Mr. Dennis,' he assured me.

'Are you sure? Because Mr. Nick and Mr. Ben have told me they have left messages for me that you haven't passed on, Mohammed,' I told him. 'They are upset with me for not returning their calls. In future, if they call please tell me so I can call them back,' I said.

'No problem Mr. Dennis, if they call and ask for you I will make a note of the time and tell you if you are not here,' he reassures me.

'Well, make sure you do,' I told him.

I made an appointment to go to see a client with Ben and when I met him, he told me Mohammed still was not passing on his messages.

'I'll talk to him again,' I promised Ben.

'He needs to understand it's important, I might have a client who wants to see you,' Ben explained.

The next time Nick came to the office, he asked me where I'd been this morning. 'I've been in the office all day so far,' I told him. He said he'd phoned and thought I was out and his messages are still not getting to me.

'Let's go and ask Mohammed why,' I said.

Nick asked him, 'Mohammed, why haven't you passed my message to Mr. Dennis?'

'What message, Mr. Nick?' asked Mohammed.

'I called this morning and asked to speak to him and you said OK, then you put the phone down on me,' said Nick.

'I know you called, Mr. Nick, but you didn't ask for Mr. Dennis,' said Mohammed.

'What! I asked to speak to him,' said Nick.

'Who?' asked Mohammed.

'Him,' said Nick, pointing at me.

'You didn't ask for him,' said Mohammed.

'What do you mean? I asked to speak to Dennis, Mr. Norman,' said Nick.

'Have you had other calls like that, Mohammed?' I asked him.

'Yes, but we don't have anyone with that name here so I ignored them, who is it?' asked Mohammed.

'Him, it's him,' Nick was shouting now and still pointing

at me.

If I didn't laugh, I would cry. I couldn't believe my ears.

'Mohammed, it is me, you should know he's asking for me, who did you think he wanted?'

'I don't know, Mr. Dennis. I have trouble hearing Mr. Nick most times because of his Scottish accent, but he definitely didn't ask for you.'

I was trying to speak without laughing my head off and apologising to Nick for Mohammed being such an idiot. I was thinking, that's what you get when you let Mosem run the hiring and firing side of the business. Between the Scottish and Egyptian accents, they had not really understood each other. That's no excuse for Ben, though; his English is very clear and his messages should have come through clearly.

'Mohammed, if any calls come through for Mr. Dennis or Mr. Norman or Dennis Norman it's me, OK, it's definitely me,' I explained to him.

'Well, I never knew that,' said Mohammed.

'For God's sake, wait until I tell Ben,' I said to Nick.

'He's going to kill him,' said Nick.

'If I don't do it first, Nick,' I agreed.

Another Trade Show

Nick was always getting invitations to trade shows all over the kingdom so he put me in touch with the organisers each time a show was planned. I wanted to be at every show possible and the first one was in Riyadh. Saud explained I needed a stamp in my iqama to allow me to travel out of the eastern province. Another Saudi rule and another cost. It would be easier if he came with me, I explained, not that I wanted him interfering but at least he spoke the language.

I couldn't do this on my own so I called Ron and asked him to help; his visit visa was still valid so he jumped at the chance. Ron always loves travelling, especially on business. Well, it is on expenses.

So we drove to Riyadh, about a four hour drive, desert all the way with one stop for a drink, and booked into the Holiday Inn Al Qasr. The show was being held in the King Saud University and there was a great turnout. We had a decent size space this time and were well prepared. No curtains needed. We certainly looked the part and were very busy from the off. Students, lecturers and the general public were much more clued up on what we had to offer. Saud had made the trip to see what all the fuss was about. He was still none the wiser but he had a few friends and relations to visit.

Due to the amount of kit we had taken, Mosem had arranged some extra help. A couple of young Filipino guys, Thomas and Julian, came to lift and carry our desks, computers and connect the electrics. They were a big help but were like the customers and kept asking questions during the show. The first day was very busy and we between us talked all day to some student or other.

During the first morning we had a call to prayer. They have five a day and this was the second of the day at mid-morning. The whole place had to be emptied and we were all told to go outside. Some religious police came round to check we'd left. I didn't want to go and leave our stand unattended with all our expensive kit on display. So I tried to stay with it. They have small sticks with trailing strands of leather at the end and they whip them around your legs so you have to be careful not to get hit. I wouldn't budge until I had covered everything. Ron asked Mosem to calm everyone down before I was arrested. In this country I just don't trust anyone when expensive equipment is involved. So we all go outside in the heat while the majority go to prayer. The heat in Riyadh was oppressing, whereas in Al-Khobar the sea breeze cooled you down. It gets to around 45 degrees in the spring time.

A highlight for me was talking to a university lecturer who ran a computer aided design course and was very interested in our software. The biggest problem was they were using unlicensed copies of all their software. I explained the need to purchase legal copies otherwise companies wouldn't be able to continue in business. How could we change their minds? My software is reliant on others so I had to make sure mine was totally legal. This would be my biggest customer if I could persuade him. Another plus was meeting the new Middle East representative for my main product. He was new to the region and he'd just taken over from Omar the Somalian, who'd been sacked for taking back handers. He was an Italian sales executive on a mission to legalise the region and his name was Gianni Leonetti. He looked like an Italian and he dressed like an Italian. His suit must have cost my month's salary, and those shoes. He wore a gold wristwatch that told the time in all the capitals of the world. What a coup for me, and little did I know how much this new found friendship would help me out in the future. I pocketed his card and vowed to keep it forever. It seemed to me you never knew what would turn out to be a good card. If this was a game of monopoly I would need a 'get out of jail free' card one day.

He came to the show every day for the week and we had lunch and dinner a few times. He explained his problems were massive as the whole kingdom was full of illegal software.

'It's more than that,' I said. 'Everything you can think of is copied from somewhere.'

Still, we received a lot of interest and had quite a few contacts to follow up when we got back to the office. We both knew the laws of piracy couldn't be enforced in Saudi Arabia. It was a closed kingdom and you couldn't apply legal pressure there. Martin was shipping my copies from London but I could get them direct from Gianni's office in Dubai now.

There's no Getting out

After about six months, things started to get to me: living on my own, in town and Seaview, the heat, the dust, moving, the fact that Saud had my passport and I was stuck there all on top of my missing the family. I was going out of my mind in the tiny studio flat on Seaview.

I missed the little things I really treasure like family, contentment, friendships, peace of mind; there was a terrible loneliness. I actually went on strike. I told Mosem to explain to Saud that if I didn't get some time off I would just stay at the compound until he agreed to let me have a week off.

Nick met Mosem before he told Saud and they arranged for me to move to a bigger place. So I moved to a three bedroom villa in Egyptian village compound. You guessed it, Mosem's idea again, always involved. They thought this would pacify me.

'The house is so empty,' I said. 'I keep walking back and forth near the telephone.'

I was talking to myself now. Everyone finds their own personal hell if they go looking for it.

There was no outlet. I couldn't keep visiting Nick and Kaitlin for company and it's not like you can go out for a drink when you want except at Neil's and there's a limit to that. There's not even a cinema. I knew that, satisfying as it might be to take my frustrations out on someone, I needed to spend my time more productively. I reconciled myself to plodding towards my goal of getting out.

School half term in England was coming up so I tried to arrange a week's leave. With Mosem translating, Saud balked, no way was he going to let me leave, it's the Arab nature not to trust anyone and Saud had put a lot of money into the business and maybe, just maybe, I wouldn't come back. So I needed someone to take my place. Keith came by and we went out for a mid-morning coffee. I mentioned I was trying to get some time off and he offered to change places with me for a week I could have his place and he would have mine and work from my office. I thanked him and said I would take him up on his offer. I felt confident that this would work so I arranged with the family for them to fly to Bahrain. In the meantime Mosem was supposedly trying to persuade Saud on my behalf to let me have my break.

I have a cousin who works for British Airways and she offered to help with the tickets. My wife told me the children were really excited about the trip and she liaised with my cousin to get the flights. The London office paid for the flights for me to help out. As the time came closer Saud was digging his heels in and refusing to budge. He didn't like the fact I was leaving Saudi, meeting my family and the prospect that I might not return. He didn't know Keith and was sceptical of our plan, even though Keith had offered to hand over his passport for the week.

So I apologised to Keith, and called Ron and Martin to discuss the situation. Keith was very nice and said I could still use his place and he would come and stay at a hotel for the week.

'We're paying for that, OK?' I offered.

Ron was going away at the same time as my planned week so it was down to Martin. At first he baulked but reluctantly agreed and said he actually looked forward to meeting Saud and trying to get us a better deal. He'd have to get past Mosem first though; good luck with that, I thought.

So we got it sorted and he would come for a couple of weeks on a visit visa so I could get a week off. When we got the faxed copy of his passport he looked like a terrorist it was so dark. My reaction was he'd fit in perfectly.

I was waiting for him at the airport and could see him through the glass as he queued at the customs desk. He looked stressed out and as he got nearer to the desk started sweating a lot. I knew it was hot but I hadn't thought I'd become that acclimatised. The customs officer opened everyone's bags and when he came to Martin, I thought he was going to faint. Hold on, I was thinking, what he has got in his luggage? He was explaining a lot to the guy and taking out clothes and folding stuff up. Anyway the customs office let him pass and he came out into the waiting area. I gave him a minute to calm down and carried his suitcase to the car.

'You told me you'd be waiting to pick me up,' he said.

'I was,' I answered.

'But I thought you'd be the other side of customs,' he said. I was actually a lot closer than anyone else could be with the help of my chief of police contact.

'I can't interfere with the customs, just the passport inspection,' I said.

'Bloody hell, I could have been locked up,' he said.

'Why, what have you done Martin?' I asked. It turned out he had porn magazines in his case.

'You're only here a couple of weeks,' I said.

He was right, though, he would have been arrested and I couldn't help him, no matter who I or Saud knew. When we got back to my place I hid the magazines, I didn't want anyone finding them and blaming me.

So after all the introductions and showing him the ropes, I thought I was going to have my week off. Be careful what you wish for. I thought it was too good to be true.

After meeting Martin, Saud seemed to be in a better mood, which pleased me because I assumed we were getting somewhere. I was readying myself to leave and the family were gearing up as well. Mosem came to me and said Saud wouldn't agree and I had to stay. To say the least I blew my top. I lost it and shouted at Mosem, saying it was all arranged and my family were getting ready to come over.

'It's just Bahrain, I'm not going back to England,' I shouted.

'He's very worried you'll go home with them,' he answered.

I didn't know what to do. Martin was trying to calm me down but I just walked out. I left them to sort something out and I walked to the beach and sat on a bench. I think that was when the whole thing started to go downhill. The trust that I thought had been building up between us just wasn't there anymore. It was all one way and it was in Saud's nature not to trust anyone.

I had to telephone my wife and explain I wasn't allowed to leave and meet her, so it was better if she didn't make the journey. She wasn't very happy, as the children were looking forward to it, but there was nothing I could do. So many plans ruined, Keith's offer, Martin's time here, we lost the flight money and they had to look for somewhere else to go in England.

I found out later it was Mosem who put the idea that I might not return in Saud's mind. I said before he'd do anything for his boss, but I didn't for the life of me think he'd do something like this. There was no way out; he had refused and I was still stuck.

Sitting on that bench, I made my mind up. There was no point hiding, I would keep looking ahead and find a way out. If Mosem could be devious, so could I.

Unless you're sure

There are a couple of contract types for people that work in Saudi Arabia. Nick had a married couple contract and his work colleague Rob had a single man contract. They both worked for an oil and gas company; Nick was in charge of the drawing department and Rob was an engineer in charge of projects. The differences in the contracts meant the company (their sponsor) would pay for Nick to bring his wife and children with him and his allowances would cater for a family. Rob on the other hand was not allowed to bring his wife, so the company wouldn't sponsor her for a visa. Therefore Nick had arranged with Saud for him to sponsor Rob's wife Mauve to become his maid, and she could live at Saud's house. This meant Rob could be with his wife as much as possible, but it was a problem because they were not seen as a married couple in the eyes of the law. Mauve was from the Philippines and Rob had married her in Manila. If they were stopped together in public they would be subject to severe punishment. Saudi laws didn't allow single men and women to be seen out together and physical contact like holding hands should be avoided.

One evening Nick and Kaitlin invited us all out to the Bangkok restaurant in town for a meal. I think it was their anniversary. Nick and Kaitlin had brought their daughter Roberta so together with Rob, Mauve, Ron and me that made seven of us. I'm not sure why I had to leave early, but the evening was rather eventful after I left. The place was quite full and service was a bit slow, but no problem, everyone was having a good time. Kaitlin went to the toilet and shortly after she came back they were all discussing the ins and outs of Saudi life when a man from the next table came over and asked her if she had seen any jewellery by the sinks in the toilets. Of course she hadn't and told him so. He complained to the manager of the restaurant who came over and asked again. The guy complaining said Kaitlin was the last person to use the toilets after his wife and she thought she had left her rings by the sinks.

'Are you accusing this lady of stealing your wife's jewellery?' asked the manager.

'Well, I'm just trying to establish if she saw them as she was the last person in there,' he saids.

'I told you I didn't see any jewellery,' said Kaitlin.

Saudi law states that if you accuse someone of a crime and it's proven they are innocent, you must be prepared to accept the punishment. The guy was reluctant to actually accuse Kaitlin of theft but was getting het up and wanted to find the rings.

The manager offered to call the police to sort out the argument but Nick didn't want to get them involved. Firstly Rob and Mauve were there and that would be disastrous, also he had whiskey and wine in his car for Saud. Ron was trying to calm the guy down and offered to search for them with him. It was a ladies' toilet and men weren't allowed to enter so they needed a woman to look. A Saudi woman from another table volunteered and came back without an answer. They were nowhere to be seen. Everyone settled down after a few minutes, but you could sense tension in the whole place now. In the meantime Mauve had taken Roberta for a walk around the restaurant to see the massive fish tank that took up the whole wall on one side of the place. She was holding Roberta up to see the top of the tank and as she went to put her down she noticed a ring on the floor by the tank. She called and the manager came and found both the rings by the edge of the tank not far from the toilet door. He returned them to their owner and warned him not to be so critical of his clientele in future.

Nick and Rob breathed a sigh of relief and thanked Mauve and Ron for saving the situation. If the police had arrived, it would have been horrendous.

Chapter 7

Get Me Out Of Here

A Birthday Surprise

In April it was my birthday; I happen to share it with the Queen and the city of Rome. This year it fell on a Friday, so luckily it was the Arabic weekend (equivalent to our Sunday), and I thought nobody knew about it so I went to the 'standard' Friday bar-b-que Ben always had at his compound. To my surprise Ben and Nick had organised a birthday party. Ron was there (I think Nick had told him to come out just to get me there), Kaitlin and Roberta were there, and to my surprise Nick had invited Neil and Simon, who brought their partners too. Ron and I arrived late morning, Nick had brought food and Neil had brought a really big cool box full of ice and drink. Ben had added a few bottles of Grolsch. Being American, Ben volunteered to cook as he said he was an expert, Ron thought the same. The biggest prawns and steaks I had ever seen but the best was his homemade sauce. It was in fact the best day I'd had so far. We all sat around the pool and had a great time until Nick threw me in with everyone singing happy birthday. My biggest surprise was that Ben had had a birthday cake made with my name on. Wow, how embarrassing. The problem with all that home brew is you're not sure how much alcohol you're getting. I obviously drank too much but I was not the only one.

Bodyguards

A short while later I really needed a break and was totally worn out, so much so that I was just going through the motions. My mental state was beginning to worry Martin and Ron so they asked our friend big Ray to see if he could bring me back to life.

My mate Ray was dying to come out and visit me as he'd never been to 'the desert' before, as he called it. There's me having a breakdown and all he wants to do is drag me up by my bootstraps and have a laugh. So he agreed to give up a summer of cricket and give it a try. They organised for him to visit for a month and help me out and my god did I need it. He even agreed to do it for a new laptop computer which he brought with him.

He's a slow right arm bowler and his team weren't very happy to lose their top wicket taker, nobody could bowl leg breaks like Ray.

After the Martin scenario he'd been warned not to bring anything illegal so we wouldn't have any hold ups at the airport.

I welcomed him by the customs hall and when he saw me he had that look on his face. 'What's going on?'

'Hi, how are you doing?' he asked.

'OK, I suppose,' I said.

'What's that "supposed" to mean?' he asked.

'Well, there's one born every minute and you're looking at him, thanks for coming,' I said.

Even though he'd been travelling for hours he wasn't tired. I think he'd stocked up on a few gin and tonics on the plane, but was 'starvin marvin' so after dropping his bags at my place we went out for some grub. I drove into town and we went to the Bangkok restaurant in the middle of Al-Khobar's main street. No problem parking, just leave your car anywhere, it's always OK; there are no parking wardens in Saudi. It's a problem attaching a parking ticket to a camel. You couldn't see the yellow lines for dust anyway.

As you pass the adjoining food outlets there are men outside with menus calling to you. They knew me by now and didn't bother me so much. They were always ready for a bit of banter, though, and enjoyed a laugh. Ray wanted to look at all the different places and menus.

'Trust me, you will enjoy this,' I said.

His eyes nearly popped out of his head when he saw the tureen of soup I'd ordered plus the main dishes.

'So tell me what's been happening in England,' I asked.

'Don't you get the news here?' he replied.

'The TV is all local news, we get some newspapers but anything political or women with bare arms they cover with a black marker pen, it's ridiculous,' I said. 'They must spend hours reading them and marking them up.'

'Well Eric Cantona got banned for eight months for kung fu kicking a Palace supporter whilst being substituted,' he said.

'No way,' I said.

'Yes way,' he said. 'The guy shouted something at him and he jumped into the crowd near the tunnel.' He knew I supported Crystal Palace and I was always interested in their news. Ray has a misguided view of English football and supported Manchester United even though he'd never been to watch them and lived over two hundred miles from their ground. In my opinion if you can't see them live you're not a true supporter. They did have the biggest fan club in the world, so maybe I was the misguided one.

He said he needed an operation on his shoulder so he was glad to rest it for a few months. There was so much to catch up on and I could have happily talked all night long; anyway I was happy for his company and someone to talk with at last. Just some noise around the place was welcoming, even his snoring.

We went to the office the next day and I introduced him to Mohammed.

'Mr. Ray is here to look after me for a while,' I told him.

'You don't need looking after, Mr. Dennis, that's what I'm here for,' Mohammed joked.

He's crap at jokes, he's never heard one before.

'He's going to come with me to clients and help with the demonstrations,' I told him.

Ray smirked and thought I was the one joking.

'Please make sure you treat Mr. Ray the same as me, OK?'

Ray said, 'You don't need me, you've got little Mo.'

'Wait a while and you'll see,' I said and I wasn't joking.

The Extension

I gave Ray the office next to me. This was Mosem's office so it was good to get rid of him for a while.

'Thanks for the window, it's alright but when you're looking out at a brick wall it's a bit depressing,' he said.

I admitted I'd seen better views. He seemed pleased though to get office to himself, but wasn't sure what he was supposed to do with it.

I called out to Mohammed to bring us some coffee and some water.

'I want white coffee, the English type with milk, not Turkish, OK?'

As soon as he turned the coffee machine on, the lights went out.

The main office was an electrical wiring nightmare because the fuses kept tripping. I assumed it was because we had a lot of office equipment and the villa had not been built to use much. The fuse box was outside the villa by the street and every time a fuse went I had to go outside to reset it. This was giving me grief because it happened quite lot.

So I thought I'd go round and check where the problems were and try to rectify them. Firstly Mohammed's office, the plug sockets were at chest height so the wiring came in at floor level and needed to be fixed to the wall up to the socket. We had an extension from a socket by the back wall coming across the floor and under Mohammed's desk. This had four plugs connected and these went to his PC, his screen, a printer and a phone/fax machine. Nearly every time he moved he kicked the extension and bang, out went the whole place.

In this country everything needed electricity. There were no gas ovens or any need for central heating, air conditioning and refrigeration were a must so you'd think they'd have a better system.

I had the back office and there were no windows and it always seemed to happen when I was sitting in my room writing quotes or on the phone to a client and the place was suddenly in darkness and the phone had gone dead, it was deadly quiet because the air con had gone off. Ray was in the front office – at least he had got a window – doing a mail merge and had hit the roof. He'll have to start again, I thought.

I went to Mohammed's desk and crawled under it to try and sort out the mess of wires. Ray came in in a rage and banged his hand on the desk. This made me jump and I banged my head under the desk. Mohammed starting crying, saying, 'You've hurt Mr. Dennis, you nasty man.' Ray almost died laughing.

Something had to be done so I called Mosem and he called an electrician, who arrived with a toolkit and drill. Ron, Ray and I went out for an hour to calm down while the work was being done.

When we came back Mohammed was lying on the floor holding a new extension against the wall behind his desk.

'What are you doing?' I ask.

'I'm fixing this new fantastic modern extension on the wall, Mr. Dennis,' said Mohammed.

'How?' I asked.

'With Blu Tack,' he said.

'Give me strength,' said Ron and grabbed the drill. 'What's this for?' he shouted. 'Hey, what's it for?'

'I don't know,' said Mohammed.

'Come on, of course you do, it's for drilling holes, so drill some and screw the extension to the wall.' Ron was almost having a meltdown. I was killing myself laughing so much I had to sit down and get a drink of water.

***

Saud arrived to check up on us. We had a small sitting room by the reception area for visitors and he used this whenever he came by. Today he had a new guy with him who sat in the reception area with Mohammed while I chatted to Saud as best I could. Mosem was away on special business for Saud so he'd brought his other minder. When they'd left I asked Mohammed who the other guy was.

'He's Mr. Saud's bodyguard, well you've got one, haven't you?'

'What are you on about?' I asked.

'Mr. Ray,' he said.

'Don't make me laugh, that guy had a machine gun under his coat. Ray's only good with a cricket bat and he definitely doesn't carry any kind of a gun.'

Thomas & Julian

I had arranged for another trade show and Ray was there to help me this time. This time we were in the King Fahd University of Petroleum and Minerals, right up my street. As my main profession was in oil and gas this would be the perfect outlet to show my stuff. I had received some new graphics cards and wanted to show them off at the next show. So we fitted one into our fastest machine and needed something to make it look good. Ray's idea was to play some of the latest movies using the computer's DVD player on our stand during the show. I wanted to show my software but it was a good way of attracting a crowd. Thomas and Julian were back to lend a hand lifting and carrying and would stay with us at my villa as I had an extra bedroom and they were used to sharing a room. We all went home after the first day setting up the stand tired out, so Thomas and Julian went to bed early. Ray was always fascinated with the Saudi TV news so he watched it most nights. The funniest thing for us was it always began with who had visited the king that day. They would show the king welcoming dignitaries from other countries queuing up to be introduced to him. It would sometimes take half an hour and all the time they would play the theme tune from the Monty Python TV show. I had asked Mosem for a television but I didn't usually watch their programs as the language was a problem. I had bought a DVD player and I could get nearly every movie produced downtown in the Shula shopping centre. Also, the aerial on the roof kept moving around on windy days, so I had a post in the middle of the lounge with a cable going up through the roof which needed adjusting every now and then.

The next day the show started at 11am so we popped into the office to check emails and the post. Mohammed or Mosem had to go to the post-box in the central post office every morning as all mail was delivered centrally and not to individuals like in the UK. They usually went before I arrived, so someone was always there for callers. Thomas and Julian were not needed today as Ray and I would do the first day and see if we needed them. So we gave them the day off. We started well and we drew the largest crowd around our stand; I gave one of my more polished routines but most just wanted to watch the film. The organisers asked us to mute the sound because we were taking all the customers away from the other traders.

A great day and much more interest than either of the first two shows.

When we came home Thomas and Julian were asleep in the lounge and when we tried to wake them they wouldn't budge. We discovered they were both unconscious, drunk. Confusion set in as I knew they were both Filipino and tee-total so they shouldn't be drinking, and where did they get it? Ray went to the fridge and saw my bottle of siddiqi had been opened and some had been drunk. I had it in an old two litre lemonade bottle with no label. Thankfully it was cut 40/60 with water. It had been full that morning.

So their first taste of alcohol and they had passed out. Maybe they thought it was water and had tried it, because they would have soon realised they didn't like the taste. Still, it's powerful stuff drank neat and it will go to your head. We left them to sleep it off and went out for a while. They were still there when we got back.

The whole week went well after that and we made a host of new contacts to follow up, and this kept me busy for a while.

***

The weekend arrived and I called Ray in from the pool. 'Come on, we're going to the beach,' I said. 'We've been invited by Neil and Simon to the British Aerospace beach.' It was private and you could wear swimming trunks or budgie smugglers in Ray's case. He looked like a body builder; all top heavy, no arse and skinny legs. Not as skinny as mine, mind you. I've seen better legs hanging out of a nest than mine in swimming shorts. It was a great way to end the week and very nice of them to allow us entry because it enabled us to get away from the Saudi rules.

We were covered from head to toe in sun cream. Ray looked like an Australian bowler with a white nose and his baseball cap on backwards.

What's that Noise?

A few days later Mohammed greeted Ray with, 'Good morning, Mr. Ray, how is London?'

'How the hell should I know, I'm here, aren't I?' he replied.

He's still got the same old wit, everyone needs a hobby. I was in the toilet and whistling 'You can call me Al' by Paul Simon to myself when I heard a commotion outside the door. When I came out, Ray and Mohammed were both in the corridor.

'What are you both doing here?' I asked.

'He doesn't know what whistling is,' laughed Ray, 'he thinks you must be a magic person.'

'What are you on about?' I asked.

'There was a funny screechy noise in there,' said Mohammed. 'Like bird had got in.'

'Was it like this?' and I whistled again.

'Yes, Mr. Dennis, how do you do that and what is it called?' he asked.

'Don't worry Mohammed, that's just me whistling,' I said.

'What is this?' he asked.

'You're joking?' I asked.

'I don't understand how you make the sound?' he asked.

Ray was beside himself and had to go to his room before he wet himself.

'Look, you purse your lips and just blow then a sound comes out, we call it whistling.' I show him how it's done and he tries but no sound comes.

'You're very clever Mr. Dennis, you must have some magic inside you.'

There's a booming laugh from Ray's office at this statement.

Later that evening Ray explains that he'd heard Mohammed in the corridor exclaiming he thought a bird had somehow got into the toilet and I was trying to catch it. Ray told him it was only me in there and that's when he said I must be magic.

Across to Jeddah

The first and the best contact from the show was Sabic. I called the Sabic representative who came to the show and he told me his office was in Jeddah. I called Mosem and said I needed to go to Jeddah and could he sort it out with Saud.

'That's in the western province,' he said. 'You can't travel outside the eastern province without a letter from your sponsor allowing you to go.'

'What! Well, I need to go, so have a word with him and make sure you tell him why, please,' I replied. 'And Mr. Ray is coming too,' I said

Ray and I went to see Saud and Mosem. Everybody in Saudi has heard of Sabic as they are into most things engineering wise.

The night before we were to fly to Jeddah we went to the Shula for some shopping. Ray couldn't believe my attitude towards the Saudi women. They were mostly covered and he couldn't see the attraction. There was one tall slim girl that particularly caught my eye.

'Look at her eyes Ray, they are Bette Davis eyes,' I said.

'What are you on about?' he said.

'You know those sultry looking come and get me eyes.'

'There's not much else we can look at,' he replied.

Her eyelashes were uncommonly long. I saw then that her eyes were a very dark brown, the darkest I have ever seen in eyes of woman or man.

'You are weird Den,' he said. 'I think you've gone native.'

He was right, I had been away too long. Anyway he wanted to buy a watch although I advised against it. So we found a booth outside one of the shops and Ray bargained with the guy and bought a fake Rolex. He seemed pleased with it anyway until it fell apart the next week. He wanted to take it back but I explained that they wouldn't take it and they'd probably deny they sold it to him at all.

Anyway we flew to Jeddah using Saudia, who were not known for their hospitality. The plane was not even half full and people were not sitting in their designated seats. When Ray and I got to our row it was already full with a family of eight across. When we complained we were told we had to move even though we'd paid for the expensive seats. So we ended up in the cheap seats well away from them near the back. We had the

Monty Python music before take-off and Ray was in hysterics. He was amazed to see women air hostesses and remarked that he thought women weren't allowed to work.

There's only one road to Jeddah and because there are no clouds to speak of, I could see the plane's shadow on the road from my window seat.

Near the end of the flight the plane banked to the left suddenly and we were all thrown to the side.

'I don't know what the pilot thinks he's doing but I just saw woman ironing in the window of that block of flats over there,' Ray shouted.

As we landed, the wheels scored the tarmac with a smoking streak before the aircraft decelerated down the long runway. You start to realise why Saudia are not in the top twenty airlines for safety. As the plane turned to loop around towards the terminal, we noted a phalanx of private jets of every description at the far end of the field. How the other half live.

We came out of the terminal to get a taxi and saw a row of about twenty waiting and a guy directing passengers towards the front of the queue. He spoke English and assured us our driver knew the place we were heading for. The language barrier was the biggest problem, the driver couldn't understand us. I showed him the business card of the person at Sabic who was expecting us and he said he knew the place. I had to trust him as I didn't really know where we were going. Anyway, you can guess what happened: we got lost. The driver was so lost he stopped at a petrol station and called someone, I gave him the card and he came back happy. When we got to the Sabic building it was the wrong one but I just wanted to get in and explain. Ray was threatening not to pay the guy as we were about forty minutes late.

Well, the receptionist arranged for us to be taken to the correct building and we eventually got to meet our guy.

Tea all round and freshen up time. I went to the toilet and there was a guy with his feet in the sink getting ready for prayer time. I had another 'what am I doing' moment.

A great guy, a great meeting and more to come it seemed. It looked like we were getting somewhere and the trip had been worth it, so far so good.

It was Ramadan and it was raining so the return journey was not even remotely easy, in fact it was farcical. We had explained why were late so the Sabic guy arranged for us to be driven back to the airport by one of the Sabic drivers. When we left it was lashing down. The driver, to give him his due, was not going to break the speed limit especially when he couldn't see the car in front of him. He told us he was from India and he'd had worse rain at home during the monsoon season. Still, we were on a tight schedule and didn't want to miss our flight. I had no idea what we would do if we missed it. We just made it though and had to hurry through check in and security, in fact we were running to the departure lounge. This time the plane was half the size and it was full, so we got our reserved seats. Monty Python played again before take-off and because of Ramadan the free food given out during the flight wasn't being touched. I told Ray not to eat his because it was disrespectful but he was starving as always. Every passenger had their tray table down with a box of sandwiches on it. Even the free soft drinks that were offered had been saved for after landing. The stupid thing is we landed with all the tray tables down, not a good idea and another reason Saudia had a bad rep for health and safety. Each passenger walked off with a box of food to be devoured at sunset, all except Ray that is.

Chapter 8

Summer

Gianni Came to Dinner

Gianni came to Al-Khobar and asked to be shown the companies I knew to be using pirated copies of his programs. I thought it was everyone, but he needed proof. I had an idea that he might be able to help me get out of Saudi and I needed him to trust me. So I organised a day out with Nick, Ben and Ron. I asked Ben if he would take the lead as he had access to virtually all companies in Jubail.

Firstly though, we were all going out to a very posh restaurant in town on the night of his arrival. Saud wanted to meet him so he chose the restaurant. He reserved a table for six at one of the best places in town, a treat for us all. I never thought they had places like this in Al-Khobar but then again I never ate more than pizza or chicken shish kebabs. Saud even wore a checked Western-style sports jacket over his dishdasha, very stylish, to say the least.

He ordered for us Saudi special slow cooked lamb and Saudi champagne. It's non-alcoholic, made from apple juice and strawberries, and it looks like Pimm's but it was very good. Good old Nick had brought a water bottle with gin in it and asked for some tonic with ice. We didn't realise what he had for a while until he offered some to Saud, who knew. I was happy with my champagne though.

Our table was positioned by the window on the second floor of the restaurant and next to us was another table with a dozen Saudi men eating. There was a screen next to them behind which was another group of diners. I asked Saud why the need for the screen so he explained the men's wives were behind there and the screen was for our benefit. We weren't allowed to see the wives and we would be offended if they were eating near us. Every now and then they would call out and one or two of the men would disappear behind the screen to sort out something.

***

The scouting party agreed to meet first thing the next day at my office and we would go in Ben's car, it being the best and the largest and he knew the way. First stop, the Saudi Iron and Steel Company, or 'Hadeed' as it was known. Ben introduced us to his contact who showed us into a conference room. Gianni explained the nature of our visit, to stop piracy in computing. His company had lost millions because of pirated software programs. We were all aware of the problems and were fighting a losing battle because we had no authority to stop it. Still, we were making people aware of it and leaving leaflets explaining the effect it was having on the industry. We carried on to a few more companies but there were so many we'd need a month just to see all in Jubail. So we headed back and when we arrived at my place we were tired out from a combination of heat, dust, talking and driving. When we had finished I was more confused than ever. I reconciled myself to plodding towards my goal of getting out. I knew I was getting somewhere but thought I'd worry about where that was when I got there.

Gianni said he had to leave but had enjoyed his time with us and would return very soon. He had to go to Qatar then onto Kuwait by the end of the week. There were plenty more larcenous contracting companies to deal with. I admitted to him I didn't envy that side of his job, just the apartment in Dubai and the film star lifestyle.

'If ever you need any help call me,' I said.

'You need to come and see it someday,' he said.

It was just what I wanted to hear.

Stuck at the Beach

Wow, what a summer we had coming; it was a scorcher. Ron was visiting and we decided to get away from the hectic traffic in Al-Khobar so the three of us took a drive us out to Half Moon Bay. As I drove the coast was on our left and the empty road ahead slowly meandered its way out of town. A silence fell, and I detected the chirping of crickets from the trees. The road goes out past the causeway bridge to Bahrain and on to a wide stretch of road with empty golden beaches going forty kilometres towards the Arabian Gulf. It seemed a shame that these wonderful beaches were not used by the locals, they were so beautiful and peaceful. Every mile or so we saw a tank on stilts near the water's edge, there were a few Saudi families having lunch under canopies and a couple on a jet ski. The lady on the back seat was totally covered in an abaya and hai', a scarf; she looked like a penguin.

We kept going as far as we could but were surprised when the road ended at a roundabout. It looked like we were in the middle of nowhere. To our left was a beach and the sand had been flattened and packed solid with cars driving on it, so we drove to the shore and parked not far from the road. The sea is so salty you can lie still and float without sinking. The temperature had soared again and after about half an hour we were so hot, we knew why this was deserted. No sensible person goes out in the midday sun. When we'd had enough we thought to try a shortcut back across the sand back to the road: bad idea. The car was a box, or an estate car in English, with the three of us and our stuff. We hit soft sand and were buried up to the doors. All four wheels were under the glorious soft sand, great for sand castles but not for driving in. We forced the doors open, got out and assessed our situation. We were about two hundred metres from the road and we were stuck. Somehow we had to dig ourselves out of this mess. We were quite near a fence and Ron broke a plank off it and started to dig under the back wheels. Ray and I were using our hands and Ron got a lot out and then used the wood to form a ski so we could try to reverse over it to safety. No luck: every time we moved a bit, the sand filled the hole. I started to wilt and Ray went to the water tank and filled his hip flask for me. We then began to realise we had been foolish going out without any water or provisions or any way to contact help. Ron must have the strength of Hercules because he kept going after Ray and I had almost collapsed. It started getting desperate and I thought I was going to pass out when we heard a car horn and looked up to the road and saw an Arab with a GMC SUV signalling to us, did we need his help? Thank the lord he came or I believe we'd be still there now. He kept a towing chain in his boot and we connected it to our front bumper and tugged us up onto the road. We couldn't thank him enough but he said he was glad to help. Ron drove us slowly back to civilisation. We stopped at the first watering hole we came across, which was a kiosk shaped like a giant fish, and drank it dry and vowed never to go out without a bottle of water again.

***

I think Mosem was jealous of me because I had befriended Gianni and he'd not been invited to the dinner with him. So one night during Ramadan he invited me and Ray to his place. He lived in a block of apartments in the cheaper side of town and I was nervous when we parked our car, there were men smoking hubbly bubbly hookah pipes in the street and in the entrance of his block by the stairs. His apartment was on the second floor and he welcomed us, introducing us to his wife Azira and daughter Kaisa, who were both lovely. They were overwhelmed to have Westerners in their home for dinner. Mosem knew a trick or two about living in this heat without air conditioning and had put silver foil over all the windows. This reflects the sun and keeps the cold inside, he explained. I don't think it works very well as I felt like I was roasting. Azira had prepared a feast for us and we looked at it sheepishly, thinking this must have cost a week's salary. Because it was Ramadan, twelve-year-old Kaisa had helped her mum with the cooking as Azira wasn't allowed to taste it before sundown.

Ray gave me the look again. 'What's going on?'

I had to give Mosem some due because he had done this for us to show he was not all bad and only did his job for Saud. He told us that evening he was really worried about his job and Azira was getting tired of him running around after Saud at all hours of the day and night. Also Saud was always asking him for alcohol, and he felt sure one day he was going to get stopped with a car boot full of whiskey. There would be no excuse; he would get deported back to Egypt and he'd never get back again.

It turned out to be a very enjoyable evening and we learnt a lot about each other. He told us Saud was a very uneducated man and his company had been left to his wife by her father and he just sort of managed it for her. That Saud was using some of her money to fund our office and he was worried that had invested too much and couldn't explain it to her. I decided to let the lads in London know first thing in the morning.

A Very Short Break

My wife was arranging our usual summer holiday and needed to know if I would be able to come. Of course I desperately wanted to be there and see my three children, so I approached Saud with a proposal. I explained it was usual in the UK to have some time away with the family during the school break. In the UK it's always the same six weeks in the summer months. Most of the expat families sent their children home for the summer as the schools packed up and the temperature was unbearably hot. There was a Saudi rule that if it reached fifty degrees you could stop work. There were pillars showing the temperature all around the city, but everyone knew they never showed more than forty nine degrees.

He promised to think about it. I told him I needed to know as soon as possible because she would be booking a package deal and they needed to know how many would be going. He'd never heard of such a thing before, his family always spent time together in each other's homes. I had flights to arrange and needed to meet her somewhere or get home before they went. Ray was still with me and wanted to come back at the same time, so we worked on Saud together. After nine months he still didn't trust me to go and come back. The only way I could leave was if Ron came and took my place for the duration of my holiday. After more discussions he wouldn't budge so I was stuck again I felt like a prisoner. Exit visas cost money and the sponsor has to agree to one and pay for it. I offered to pay my own this time to smooth the way. Ron knew I wanted to get out, if only for a couple of weeks, and he swung it with his wife to relieve me. He didn't like going on holiday during school breaks anyway, too many kids around. Neither did Ray. So Ron and I arranged flights to and from Heathrow and I prepared myself for a vacation.

He arrived and Ray and I were ready to go. The problem was, Saud still couldn't bear the fact I had managed to wangle some time away. He kept us waiting and when he eventually arrived at the office with my passport he still wanted to keep me there. It was late afternoon and our flight was at eight o'clock. Ray was getting anxious; our flight time was getting close, Ron was there, we had to leave for the airport and Saud was making excuses. Couldn't he see we had kept our side of the bargain?

Saud's problem was Ron could leave anytime he wanted because he was on a visit visa, whereas I had a work visa and needed Saud to allow me to go. Mosem was trying his hardest to persuade him and eventually he gave in when Ron gave his word he would stay until I came back. I had left Ron a lot to follow up and he would be busy.

Buddy drove me and Ray to the airport and we caught an Air France flight to Heathrow via Paris. The first thing I wanted on the plane was a real gin and tonic. The air stewardess said she understood as they flew that route quite a lot. Absolutely wonderful; I was out.

While we waited for our connecting flight in Paris they announced, 'Anyone for Nantes.'

Ray immediately piped up with, 'We've been in Saudi for months so probably yes.'

'It's spelt N-A-N-T-E-S, not nonce,' I said.

The Last Few Months

When I got home, virtually everyone told me to stay there. That was never going to happen. As far as I was concerned, Ron was the prisoner now and he had helped me out when I asked. Not everyone gets the life they want. I had a duty to go back and allow Ron to come home for the holiday he had postponed. Also to show Saud I was committed and was trustworthy. I had my own plans for getting home without Saud realising I was gone. So after my fortnight off, I went back to work.

I missed Ray so I concentrated on the office work. September was busy. I didn't expect Ron for a month or two, but Ben was on hand to keep me sane and we went together to Al-Jubail and tried to drum up some business. There were plenty of companies to visit so we kept at it and eventually we got a result. Sabic were into most things. Founded in 1976 by royal decree, they were now ranked among the world's largest petrochemical manufacturers. It is owned by the government, and they were ripe for our products. I always had my laptop with me fully loaded and ready for any demo. All I needed was a screen, which most companies were able to supply. Ben was a good salesman and left the technical stuff to me and between us we managed to persuade them to ask for a quote. That's a result in my book. A quote from Sabic is as good as money to me. After a bit of haggling we made a sale and it turned out to be my last.

Mohammed continued being stupid but one morning when I arrived at the office he had been crying. He'd written me a letter explaining how sad he was and how Mosem hated him. He hated living at the back of the office and thought he deserved better accommodation. He wanted to move closer to his friends so he could see them more often. He always ended up walking home late at night because they lived so far away. He said Mosem wouldn't allow it, saying we wouldn't pay out for a place for him while where he lived was OK.

'It's all right for him, he's got his family here and he lives in an apartment in town,' he said.

It made me think of my old apartment and wouldn't offer that to my worst enemy. I felt sorry for him and asked him why he came to Saudi Arabia.

'I came to get a better job and to get money so I could send some back for my parents,' he replied.

'OK, those are worthy reasons, but we have to manage our money as well,' I told him. 'We have expenses like you and we have a budget to maintain, if we spend some of that on rent for your accommodation then we can't spend it elsewhere.

'Your rent would mean less to go round and possibly less for all of us and you wouldn't want that, would you? Not only that, you'd have to get here in the morning and that would mean getting up really early. At least now you're never likely to be late for work. If you lived in town I guarantee you'd meet your mates more, spend more and sleep less,' I told him.

And be more dozy then you are now, I thought to myself.

'Then you'd have less money to send home and I'd be

worried about you as well. Stop getting upset, you've nearly done a year and then you can have a break with your family. I'll have a word with Mosem for you,' I told him.

Mosem needed to understand I needed Mohammed to be at his best, because any worse and he might as well go home now.

The Last Show

In late September I'd been there almost eleven months when I received a call from Gianni Leonetti about a trade show in Dubai. A thought in my head said maybe, just maybe, this could be my 'get out of jail free' card. As I was now regarded as the leading dealer for his products in Saudi Arabia's Eastern Province, would I like to be part of their presence at the show? This was the largest show on the planet by far and I wanted in. I had this strange little feeling of… some kind of unholy joy. Every once in a while an electric sparkle, like knowing you're soon to go on holiday. From little acorns great forests grow and my assessment of the invitation was that we were going to get a lot of sales after this show. I told Mosem and he thought Saud would object. I told him I thought it was just what we needed and would freshen up the company with a broader sales outlook. We approached Saud and Mosem translated for me that we needed to go. As far as Mosem was concerned Saudi was massive enough and we should concentrate here. There would be Saudis there, I told him, and they would find us. We would never find so many people from my little office. I left with Mosem and knew I needed him on my side to persuade Saud. It would be touch and go; I needed an exit visa.

I could see a way out but needed the guys in London to help. I'd heard that people travelling to Israel needed a visa in their passport and if you had one you were barred from Saudi. I wasn't sure if it was true, probably not, but I so wanted to get home. I contacted Martin and explained my dilemma. He thought he could sort it but it might take some time. Not too long, I hope. Ron was thrilled to hear of Gianni's offer and wanted to promote the London office at the same time. So he organised his trip to Dubai before I had even got Mosem on my side. I had a month to work on him and it took the first week to sweet-talk him into it. He was suspicious as I'd not always got on that well with him. It took me a couple of lunch invitations and a few coffees in the Shula to get him listening to the virtues of Dubai. I felt my persuasion was paying off because he invited me to his place to meet Azira again at the weekend and I went. During the evening I asked him why he doesn't want me to go to Dubai.

'It's not that, it's what Saud wants,' he said. I knew secretly he wanted to go for a week and have a drink or two while he was there.

'Bring Saud and we can all have a nice time, it will be like a holiday for you two,' I tell him.

I'm sure he wasn't aware the week would be so relaxing for him. They would both be in a hotel and could chill out from the harsh life they were used to. Anyway he relented and assured me he would try his best to get Saud round to my way of thinking. The next day I told Gianni I would love to come, and he booked a room for me in the Princeton Hotel with his team. I called Ron and he booked himself in the same hotel. I was still not convinced I was going, but it was nice to set things in motion. The second week I was out and about with Buddy and trying to forget about it while closing a few deals. I didn't have to set up anything for the show as Gianni assured me they had everything I was going to need, so no pressure there. I left Mosem to work his magic and hoped for the best. When he came to see me next he had good news. Saud was going for it and would finance the whole trip.

I had a few things I wanted to do before I went, so I bought a couple of hard disks and swapped them with the two machines in the office.

I wasn't sure if I was coming back, so I packed everything I needed, including the old hard disks, and left behind what I could do without.

Mosem had booked the flights via Bahrain and Buddy took us to the airport on the Friday morning before the show started. At the airport check-in desk Saud had my passport and kept it with him for the whole journey. We changed at Bahrain and I waited in the lounge while they went to duty free to buy some booze. That's if you can call it duty free. When they returned I was amazed how much they were allowed to buy. It looked like no limit between countries, unlike in the UK where the limits are quite small. They had bought about a million cigarettes each as well. Saud asked me to carry some of his bottles to share the load. When we arrived in Dubai it was like a breath of fresh air. The tension in my body just lifted and I felt free. What an amazing feeling. When we landed Saud handed me my passport so we could pass through customs and then he asked for it back. I gave it to him to keep from arguing. A cab to the hotel and my reservation was there and I checked in. They asked to copy my passport information so Saud had to give it up; they would give it back later that day. Saud tried to check in and was refused. I couldn't believe it – the hotel was full. Mosem hadn't bothered to check. They had to go to another more expensive but very plush hotel on the other side of town. I gave them my room number and they left. I went up to my room and called reception to ask for Ron's room number. I called him and we met in the coffee bar downstairs.

'I've got a present for you,' he said.

'What?' I was so pleased to be out I was not really listening. He gave me an envelope and inside was a brand new UK passport.

'Oh my god, thank you so much.' I was nearly in tears from relief.

'Don't thank me, thank Martin, he organised it'

'How on earth did you get it?'

'Your idea of travelling to Israel worked, he explained it to the passport office and they agreed it could be awkward so they issued you with a second one, it runs along with your first one and expires on the same day.'

Talk about happy; I was ecstatic now. Let's go and meet Gianni and buy him a drink.

The next day Ron and I went to the show and looked in awe at the impressive stand we were to exhibit at. Gianni introduced us to dealers from Dubai and Abu Dhabi in the UAE, Bahrain, Qatar, Oman and Kuwait. I'd never been to such a big show, and to be part of it was impressive. The week went well and Saud didn't bother us much after visiting once to have a look and wanting introductions. I'm still convinced he didn't see the need. I enjoyed myself and showed a lot of people how good our products were.

At the end of the week Ron and I went to see Saud and Mosem at their hotel for a drink and a meal.

I showed them the amount of interest people had shown and left business cards, and I wanted to follow them up as soon as possible. I asked Saud to stay another week so we could visit some of the places in Dubai and Abu Dhabi. Saud refused and wanted me to return with him immediately. I was completely being honest with him and would have returned after another week but he was being unreasonable and controlling. This made my blood boil again and I said to Ron on the way back to our hotel I was going to book a flight back to the UK in the morning. So I did and took it. Saud still had my original passport and he could keep it for all I cared. I was home for good with my family and friends at last. Or so I thought.

Anyway as the saying goes, yesterday is history.

Part 2

Chapter 9

Come Again?

On June 25, 1996 the Khobar Towers, a US Air Force housing complex, was bombed by militants. It was a terrorist attack on part of a housing complex in the city, located near the Aramco headquarters and the nearby King Abdulaziz Air Base . At that time, Al-Khobar Towers was being used as quarters for coalition forces who were assigned to Operation Southern Watch , a no-fly zone operation in southern Iraq, as part of the Iraqi no-fly zones.

A truck bomb was detonated adjacent to Building number 131, an eight-storey structure housing members of the United States Air Force 's 4404th Wing , primarily from a deployed rescue squadron and deployed fighter squadron. Nineteen U.S. servicemen and a Saudi local were killed and four hundred and ninety eight of many nationalities were wounded. The official June 25, 1996 statement by the United States named members of Hezbollah Al-Hejaz as responsible.

Going Back

I couldn't believe it: he did it again.

I'd been back in the London office for a few months when Nick called me again and asked me to come back.

'You've got to be joking. Oh no,' I said.

After the latest attack in Al-Khobar I wasn't keen to say the least.

'This had better be good.'

'No, listen, this is totally different. I've changed my job, I'm the new manager at Arabscan,' he said. 'You remember them from a few floors down in my office block? Well, I need some help,' he explained. 'Come on, I need a technical assistant, someone who's good at IT and can be wing man.' He was pleading now.

'I'm not allowed back, I'm black listed at the chamber of commerce,' I told him.

'I've checked that and you're OK with your new passport,' he said.

'I'm not going through all that palaver again with my new squeaky clean passport, anyway they wouldn't let me in,' I said.

'Look, I've had a word with my new bosses and explained your situation and they are willing to talk to Saud and get you in,' he explained.

'After the way I left, he'll have me arrested,' I said.

'Not necessarily, he's not that bad. He likes me and we'll get him off your back.'

'And how are you going to keep him there?' I asked.

'Will you consider it if I can get a letter from Saud saying he's got no problem with you coming back and working with me?' he asks.

'OK, I'll put it to the family first then if, and it's a big if, they are OK with it then and only then I'll tell the partners at work.' That was all I was prepared to do.

'I don't want to know the ins and outs until you send me a signed letter from Saud,' I told him.

It goes without saying I couldn't concentrate for the rest of the day. I went home and discussed it. I pointed out it would be different this time.

He sent me an email outlining the job description. He made it sound very different from my last attempt at living there. This time I wouldn't be on my own trying to find sales and traveling to a lot of unknown places. I'd be more office bound or out with him. He'd be the point of sale and I'd be technical backup. It sounded much better suited to me.

It meant I'd have to temporarily leave the partnership, as no sales would be going through their office unless it was their direct products.

He must be very persuasive because after a couple of days he called and said he'd sorted it out and I would be getting an email with a document attached signed by Saud. It arrived the next day and I printed it to show anyone who was interested. Boy, was this a massive weight off my mind, even if I didn't go back. Just to get Saud off my back was amazing; how had he managed it? I wondered.

It must be obvious from the writing of this book that I accepted his latest offer and went back.

Again I was pretty excited but for different reasons. I had liked what little I remembered of Arabscan and their whole setup.

While I started closing down my side of the partnership, Martin helped with the courier service he'd used for my new passport to get my second visa. I didn't want to show my face at the Saudi Arabian embassy again as long as I lived. I finished all the courses I was running and had a week off before I planned to go.

Nick phoned again.

'Would you mind going to the States for some scanner training before you come here?' he asked. 'You'll have to organise it yourself and we'll reimburse you when you get here,' he explains.

Talk about getting excited, this was unreal.

'Hold on, this sounds a bit dodgy,' I said.

'Trust me, it's all OK. They're expecting you and I've had the OK from here,' he promises.

'Trust you, that's a laugh. Well, maybe just this one time.' Ha ha.

Oh my god, the States, what was I going to pack? Holy moly, my credit card will take a bashing here, I thought. I was booking direct this time, no agencies.

Go West then East

So I planned a two week trip. Fly to Philadelphia via New York for a week and then onto Denver for another week then straight to Dhahran. I didn't know where each of the offices were, so I picked the first hotel at random and hoped for the best. I'd just get the first flight out of the way and when I got there I'd get an internal flight to and from Denver. This was my first visit to America, and I was buzzing inside. I was so excited I couldn't sleep in the few days leading up to it or on the plane going over.

I had a bit of a scare at the check-in desk at Heathrow because they queried my Saudi visa. They asked me who I worked for, and for how long. I said I'd not started yet and was going for training before starting my new job. I was made to wait until they checked my passport out. I'd never flown this far west before but I'd been told to set my watch forward to the country time where I was going so my mind would adapt to the arrival time quicker, so I did and it kind of worked.

It didn't occur to me that it was the 4th of July weekend when I arrived in Philadelphia and I had no idea how this would affect my trip. Firstly, my hotel was right across town and miles away from the place where my training was being held. Secondly, the cab from the airport took an age to get there and charged me a small fortune. After checking in I arranged my return flight to Denver for the following weekend. I'd thought internal flights were bound to be cheap, but not if you booked within a seven day notice. I spent the weekend getting over the jetlag, it had really affected me.

The first company I had to visit was Scangraphics, who made the biggest paper scanners in the world. I called their office on the Monday morning and asked the best way to get there.

'Why are you staying there? You need to move closer, it will take you forever each morning to get here otherwise,' their receptionist said.

She gave me a list of hotels closer and I picked the closest, which just happened to be the most expensive. The problem was the World Series end of season baseball game was being played in the city and every reasonably priced hotel was full. I checked out, grabbed a cab and moved across town. I'd already spent the cash I'd allocated for the week on two cabs.

This meant the first morning was wasted while I moved. Still, I wanted to get going and was ready by lunchtime. The guy who came to get me modelled himself on the John Travolta character from *Saturday Night Fever* and had an all-singing all-dancing red Cadillac with cream leather seats and a big engine to go with his big ego. He was very flash and liked to show off his clothes and haircut, wide lapels and all. I couldn't believe it but the first thing we had to do was stop. I was just getting going and we have to stop.

'Starbucks,' he said.

'What's Starbucks? I don't think we have them in England,' I told him.

'Breakfast, coffee and donuts.' He was either trying to impress me or he was actually hungry.

I could have done with some lunch but I wasn't going to argue with this mafia guy.

When we finally arrived at the office he showed me their scanners and at 80 inches across I'd never seen some this big before, and at first wasn't sure what to make of it. The rest of the team were really helpful and the training went better than I expected.

'John Travolta' collected me every morning and dropped me back every night. The rest of the team took it in turns to take me out each evening, reluctantly I think, but they were very nice. Every meal was a mountain of food, which was a lot compared to my usual. I finished the training on the Friday and they presented me with a certificate; it hadn't felt like training and I didn't think I'd passed an exam so it was very nice and another thing to add to my CV.

I had Saturday and Sunday off so I took the round town trolley bus and saw the sights. I saw the Liberty Bell and went to Independence Hall, where the Declaration of Independence and Constitution were signed. It is a wonderful city with a great history.

On Monday morning I caught a United flight to Denver. I was being collected by someone from a company called ANAtech. I'd already phoned ahead and was expecting to be met by the car hire at the airport. There was a slight delay with the flight so I ended up landing around a half hour late. I collected my luggage and rushed to the meeting place and was surprised to find nobody waiting for me. I waited for a further half an hour but when no one showed I called them. I was told the guy was already back at the office as I hadn't shown up.

'The plane was delayed, surely he would have checked that?' I said. 'Never mind, what shall I do then?'

'You'll have to rent a car,' they said.

That was the last thing I wanted to do. I'd never driven in the States before, where is 'John Travolta' when you need him? He was five hours away in another state.

Still, there was no other way as my lift wasn't coming back for me.

I saw the queues for at the car rental desks and joined the Hertz queue.

A lady in Hertz uniform came over to me.

'Do you have a reservation sir?' she asked.

'No, I've just been advised to rent a car as my driver hasn't arrived.'

'Well, you won't get one here or any of the others with lines.'
'Why?'
'Because everyone has reserved in advance and we cater for whose coming and no more, you could go to the "Record" guys over there their desk has no line.'

OK, so why don't they have any customers, I thought to myself.

'Do you have any cars left?' I asked at the Record desk.
'Yes, but can you drive a stick shift, sir?' the lady asked.
'What's a stick shift?' I asked.
'One with gears and a gear stick by the seat,' she said.
'Do you mean a manual car?' I ask. 'Of course I can, I'm English.'
'I thought I recognised your accent, yeah we got one left.' She's blushing now.

So we completed the paper work and I was given a map. Fat lot of good that was, I had no idea how to get out of the airport let alone which was north or south. The car ended up being the smallest Hyundai they make. With all the massive cars you see around, it was like a toy. I walked around it and found the dent in the back bumper that they'd not noted on the sheet. I went back and got the attendant and pointed it out then we both had a good look at it, then he marked it on both copies of the sheet. The people who scrape them toss the keys in and get on the plane. I couldn't blame them for not letting the office know, everyone's in a rush these days. My dad taught me to inspect the cars I hired and read the small print. In these matters I am like my old man. One day I'll wake up inhabiting my father's body and it won't be a shock.

I was straight back on the phone again asking directions and they made it sound straight forward. Get on the main highway going south for ten miles, and when you see the Holiday Inn turn right, and we're two roads down on the right.

That was another Monday morning of missed training. It was lunchtime when I got there and as I was booked into the Holiday Inn they send me straight back to check in and grab some lunch. I was having a bad day so it was no surprise when I got back to the car and it wouldn't start. After a couple of tries I went back and asked for help. The receptionist came out and it started at the first go.

'Don't look so embarrassed, you have to put your foot on the clutch before it will start with stick shift cars,' she said.

'We don't have that in England.'

'Well, in the States everyone drives an automatic, so if we get a stick shift that's left in gear it will jump forward if we don't push the clutch,' she explained.

It was my turn to look and feel stupid so I offered thanks and headed off to the hotel to check in. I was starving so anything would do for lunch, and the nearest place was a Wendy's burger bar. So I was already eating junk food and I'd only been in Denver for a few hours; there were unlimited refills for Pepsi too.

When I got back I met all the technical staff and they showed me their scanners. Also they offered me a ticket to the local baseball game that night.

'It's the Rockies against the Giants,' I was told. 'That's Colorado verses San Francisco.'

'Yes please, who is going?' I asked.

'Nobody can go so this ticket is going spare. You can have it if you want.'

'That's amazing, thanks a lot. I'm OK as long as someone gives me directions to the stadium, it's my first day driving in your country, but at least I can start the car now.' I was thrilled and the game was fantastic.

In fact the whole place was great and I met another English guy who had been sent there for a month to help out and stayed for five years, eventually marrying a girl from Denver.

Nick called me halfway through my training course at ANAtech to ask if I would mind living with him and Kaitlin. I was entitled to a twenty five percent increase for accommodation costs this time and Nick proposed combining ours and living together in Bahrain. What a result. Living in Bahrain made me feel so much better than living in Saudi.

'I'm up for that,' I agreed.

He'd put a proposition to the two Arabscan owners that we rented a villa in Bahrain rather than two places in Al-Khobar. In his opinion they should want to show their clients that they were a forward thinking company and trust their managers to live outside the Kingdom. I was not in a position to argue and agreed, especially as we would be living in Bahrain. This meant I would keep my passport to allow me to pass into Saudi every morning to work and out again after work. Amazing, maybe my luck was changing, but I had a long way to go yet.

Again I had the Saturday off before my trip to Dhahran. Denver was a place I'd always wanted to go and it brought back childhood memories of watching Western shows on TV. I asked at the hotel reception where I could spend the day. They advised I drive into Boulder as there was a Wild West show in the main streets. People dressed up as cowboys and Indians in a pageant from the old days. As I drove to town I passed a sign for Central City, which I thought meant the centre of the city of Boulder, so I followed it. The road kept going uphill for miles and I saw people panning for gold in the river by the roadside on my way up. I drove for about half an hour and ended up in 'Central City.' This was a gambling town and every shop was a small casino. Men in tall hats and women in bonnets were carrying buckets of loose change up and down the streets going to each place to play the slot machines. I was so hungry I found a diner and ordered a steak. it was so big it reminded me of a *Tom and Jerry* cartoon sketch with those T-Bone steaks bigger than them.

It was a massive journey for me when I left Denver. I needed to fly to Philadelphia then on to New York then to Heathrow then on to Dhahran. Still, I managed to get into the British Airways lounge at Heathrow so a bit of luxury along the way. It was nice to be able to call my wife and I spoke to my children and my mum. My credit card had indeed taken a bashing.

Arabscan

When I arrived in Dhahran for the second adventure it was very different from the first. I had to queue with the other passengers and have my passport checked thoroughly. I was dreading it and worried sick that they would pick up on my last visit. It went smoothly, in Saudi terms, and Nick met me again but this time in the arrivals hall.

This was a completely different story because I had a year's contract of employment and a salary with living allowance and accommodation. Nick had booked me into Le Meridian on the corniche right by the beach. It looked and felt like a Royal Palace with Rolls Royces, Lexuses, Crown Victorias, Ferraris and SUVs parked in the car park and the air smelt like sweet perfume.

I knew the rules now and had no qualms about having to stay there for a week while the necessary paperwork was prepared, a bit like chalk and cheese.

Nick came for lunch on my first day and we chatted about things that had happened while I had been away. Both our worlds seemed to be in a mess; there had been a bomb in Manchester and a bomb in Al-Khobar. The Olympics were on and all the Western newspapers had women athletes blacked out with felt pen to stop people seeing their bare arms or legs.

'They thought the king was dying a little while ago so he transferred power to Crown Prince Abdullah,' Nick told me, 'but he got better and got it back a few months later.'

'Blimey, I can't imagine Prince Charles becoming King of England, even temporarily,' I said.

My new office was in the tallest building in Al-Khobar and we had the complete fourth floor, a hundred percent different from the small villa. Nick had taken over around six weeks before I arrived and had divided his office into two to make space for me. We were positioned next to the owners' office at the head of the main open plan office.

Arabscan was owned by Mr. Mohammed Al-Rebdi, and Mr. Mosen Al-Belali, two very different guys who between them ran a tight ship. Mr. Belali was a morning person and Mr. Rebdi arrived for the afternoons.

It seemed a bit strange to me why this was, but on that first day as I looked at Mr. Rebdi more carefully I realised he was drunk. He seemed to have the control of a practised drinker, awareness of his limitations and automatically compensated for it. I wasn't sure how but I knew then that the two partners were avoiding each other and only met for important meetings.

Mr. Belali disagreed with Mr. Rebdi's drinking so they had made the morning/afternoon deal.

Nick explained that even though Mr. Belali and Mr. Rebdi didn't know so many local prominent people like Saud did, they had been to university with quite a lot of government officials. They had been to the USA for education and learnt with people from Bahrain and Kuwait, Qatar and the UAE. They had both sent their sons there as well. They were still good friends with many of them.

I was introduced to the receptionist, called Hamid, and I found out after a while that he ran the office underground. I was shown around and met the staff, around twenty in the office and overall there were over fifty people. Mac was from the Philippines and managed the main drawing office with a team of a dozen designers. Jaime was a programmer, also from the Philippines, there were couple of scanner operators, a driver, and then there was Gopal the office dogsbody. We also had a Lebanese salesman called Suliman who spent every day driving around visiting clients. Nick explained we had other people working at various client offices as well, and we would be visiting them during the week.

On my second day Nick, Mr. Belali and Mr. Rebdi had arranged a meeting to discuss some proposal they were planning for the company. They explained they had already been in contact with people in Bahrain, Kuwait, Qatar and the UAE and were planning a meeting in our office with a representative from each company.

Nick was a shrewd guy and wanted to use all my old contacts from my business with Saud to make Arabscan not only the biggest dealer in office scanners in the whole Middle East but computer aided design as well. He'd been in charge of a similar office and knew how difficult it was to find a good supplier. He asked me to contact Gianni Leonetti and propose the joint venture. I was to be the technical manager and they would use my expertise to promise good backup. As opposed to our competition who employed people from the Philippines or India; his words, not mine.

Our main software competitor was a company called Bentley. Nick wanted them as well and proposed we deal in both. Their representative for the region was a welsh man called Owen. He used to visit Nick at his last company so Nick had invited him to visit us to see if we could become a dealer. He had obvious reservations because we were selling his main rival's product. That was until we persuaded him we could back it up and offer both. Either would suit us and it always depended what the customer had or wanted. There wasn't much support for either product outside anyway. We needed a super tech person to convince him. He left without giving us an answer and promising to come back in a month. We needed to get someone on board by then.

We'd both met quite a few expats since arriving two years ago and one guy was working for a company that sold the rival product. He knew that our main competitor had the dealership but he'd become quite friendly with their main tech support guy. He was a Filipino called Donde and Nick suggested we offer him a better job with us.

Nick's answer to all problems was, 'If you can't beat them, buy their centre forward.' That's typical of an engineer, always looking for and usually finding an angle.

Together we spoke to Mr. Belali and Mr. Rebdi, who knew we would have a problem as he couldn't just leave and jump ship to join us. Still, Nick wouldn't leave it there so he asked Donde to think about it and in the meantime we would come up with a solution. So we racked our brains and soon we had our solution. Mr. Belali knew people in Kuwait with a similar company and possibly could take him for the six months needed before he could come back, if he decided to go for it. Mr. Belali called them and they agreed to help out. So we put it to Donde and he wanted a week to consider and talk to his girlfriend about it. After a week we had a meeting and he had decided he wanted to do it.

His girlfriend Lia had to leave at the same time or he wouldn't go. We arranged it for the next month and waited for the company in Kuwait to come back to us with a written agreement.

Another thing about Saudi Arabia is the way small companies or consultants worked with the major companies like Aramco and Sabic. Every two years the consultancies would bid to be added to a preferred list of a dozen companies that could work for the majors. Once you were included on a major company's preferred list, you knew they had to provide you with some work in the next two years. All the big companies worked like this and it was part of my job to make sure we were on as many lists as possible.

We got stuck in and visited loads of companies trying to get some work for our company, or if not, interest them in buying their own equipment. Nick assigned me an assistant who looked after the main office machines, his name was Matthew.

We had contracts with a few companies to supply men to work in their offices.

Chapter 10

Bahrain

Now that's Better

Nick was unable to rent a place in Bahrain for us as he and I were supposed to be living in Saudi. Luckily one of our new bosses had been to school with a Bahraini guy who did us a favour and sponsored Kaitlin to rent a villa in her name.

Our villa was brand new and fantastic with four bedrooms, two with en-suite, a family bathroom and a massive kitchen/dining area. It had a really big lounge with concealed ceiling lighting, a huge tiled entrance hall with a chandelier and a solarium on the roof. The compound had a kidney-shaped pool with a bridge across to a waterfall with a slide. There was a fully fitted gymnasium.

It was on a small newly built compound near the coast with fifteen other villas. A little bit of paradise amongst the unrest in the Middle East. Plus we were getting a maid to live in, there was a small room for servants by the kitchen. Nick and Kaitlin interviewed a couple and settled on a 'lady', that's my opinion anyway, from Sri Lanka who also in my opinion was a princess. She was called Mira and had two daughters back home who she missed a lot. She looked after us and was a great cook as well.

'How on earth did you manage this?' I asked Nick.

'This is to make up for all the crappy places you've lived in this past year,' he said. 'I persuaded Rebdi and Belali they needed a strong leadership team to run Arabscan and they both agreed, so I proposed this and explained the need for trust or it wouldn't happen.'

So Nick and I combined our accommodation money and Arabscan paid the total year's rent up front; it must have been around twenty thousand pounds. Just goes to show how much Nick was earning. I had my own room with an en-suite bathroom and we shared the communal areas.

The only problem I could see was it was unfurnished, and I wasn't prepared to pay for furniture in a place that big out of my salary. Nick knew I had a house back home with a mortgage, so I wasn't going to be splashing money around on luxury stuff. He helped me out by buying my bed and he furnished the rest. To start with I had a futon bed but I changed it after a few weeks.

It's not all paradise, though, because once a day a camel herder brought his herd of camels by our main entrance and the smell was awful. You could check your watch by him. He passed the same time every day with about a dozen camels.

Bahrain and Saudi Arabia are separated by the Gulf of Bahrain. The Saudis and Bahrainis built a causeway bridge from Al-Khobar in Saudi to Al Jasra in Bahrain. There is a customs building halfway along, nicknamed passport island, where you need to show passports and have your luggage checked.

Our villa was not far from the bridge, so Nick and I could get on it before the rush most days. We had to drive the 26km across the causeway to the office every morning and back every night so we had been issued with a bridge pass. This was a small booklet with 30 pages, each page divided into four, lasting a month for both passport offices on the bridge to stamp each time. Passing through two sets of customs each way, now that's a lot of stamps, and everyone's passport would soon be filled with stamps otherwise.

Mr. Rebdi had persuaded Mr. Belali to let us use a company car, a Hyundai Sonata – still no Rav4 – which we shared, and we were both allowed to take our laptops with us. It really was a different world getting out every night and driving home, as I called it, singing along to The Lighthouse Family hit 'Ocean Drive'.

How things change, I hear you say.

A beautiful island

Bahrain had become independent from Britain in 1971 but was still favourable to British citizens.

Once passing through customs you could stay for ninety days from the day your passport was stamped. This meant I could come and go as I pleased as I was going in and out each day, unlike last year, keeping my British passport with me at all times.

The big difference between living in Bahrain and living in Saudi was there's always something to do. There's a cinema with movies in English and tons more Western restaurants and food outlets. There was a country club with pools and gymnasiums with bars and alcoholic drinks. Not far from our compound was a new style food court with eating outlets all around a large seating area. Our favourite was a pizza place with large pizzas the size of dustbin lids, great for sharing.

There's a horse racing course and the gambling laws were relaxed. They had a tote for small bets. There were the obvious illegal bookies offering any bet you wanted, but all done quietly and undercover from the police. They also had broadband internet available, so we signed up for a years' contract. A least I could read the English newspapers online and check the football results. I found a site called 'CPFRIS' that posted weekly match reports about my favourite team Crystal Palace.

***

After we'd been there about a month, Kaitlin announced she was pregnant.

Nick was so excited he bought her a new car, a Renault Clio. She was so excited because she'd not been able to drive in Saudi. The first weekend after it arrived, she wanted to go exploring.

'Come on, we're going out for the day,' Kaitlin said one Thursday morning.

'Where?' I asked.

'The Amir has a private beach and he allows people to spend time there,' she answered.

That's Isa bin Salman Al Khalifa, by the way. He had a house on the beach at the bottom end of the island and the gardens around it were open to the public. We could go there at the weekend and were allowed to sunbathe and swim. There was also a small café where you could get free soft drinks, tea or coffee. The weather was always balmy, hot or warm and the sea was calm with hardly any waves. As we drove we passed the 'Tree of Life' which is the only tree for miles around. It stands all alone on a small hill and is fenced off from tourists who used to try and cut branches off it. It is amazing how this one tree has survived for over 400 years in the middle of a desert with no water around or any other living thing for miles. We passed a wildlife reservation with wild animals, like a safari park to drive around. It would be the ideal place to take my wife and three children when they visited during half term from school. So I made a mental note to organise a family visit.

Even though I thought Bahrain was a little paradise and a nice place to live, the Bahraini people weren't happy with so many expats living and working there or the regime. There had been unrest during the whole of the 1990s and some called it the uprising of dignity. The main aim was democratic reforms; there had been around forty civilians' deaths during the '90s so far. I got a shock one night as I drove into town some local guys were throwing blazing tyres from the back of a flatbed truck into the road in front of me. I had to steer round the flames to avoid hitting the tyres. It was unnerving and made me think everywhere has its problems.

So many Differences

We were driving into Saudi to work and we heard on the British forces radio that Osama Bin Laden had issued a call to remove the American military from Saudi Arabia. They were calling it a fatwa, whatever that was.

'Is that the same Bin Laden we have work for in Riyadh?' I asked Nick.

'We have dealings with the Bin Laden Group, it's a big family,' he said.

'Holy moly, it's scary when you think we have dealings with them,' I said.

'We're quite safe in Dhahran,' he said.

'But that's where the Americans are, aren't they?' I asked.

'Stop worrying, it's not going to affect us,' he assured me.

'It's in my character to worry, I was born worrying,' I said.

'Well, stop, and that's an order,' he said.

'OK boss.'

I was expecting a call from my mum any day now.

We had lot nationalities working at Arabscan. All together we had Saudi, Bahraini, Filipino, Thai, Indian and Pakistani, oh and British as well. Some were Catholic, some were Muslim, some were Christians, and a couple were Sikhs. When I joined I had no idea which was which and this caused me some embarrassment during my stay. Muslim prayer time would affect most of the team. But the others didn't pray so often and didn't fast during Ramadan. The Filipinos were the best because they were all mates and didn't cause any upsets. Indians had caste matters as well as religious ones. All of our Pakistanis were Sunni Muslim but I never found out about the Saudis or Bahrainis. I got a few things wrong when putting teams together and learnt about age versus religion. It was a massive learning curve for me and a mountain to climb. It was like the League of Nations.

A dozen of the Indian and Pakistani boys had a smart way of saving. Every month they each put a thousand riyals into a pot together with all their names, then they drew out a name and he got the twelve thousand to send home. Each month they drew another name minus the previous winners. One such winner called Sreejith Pillai sent his money home and his brother opened a small office to offer training for future Arabscan designers.

A new Indian driver had arrived with me in July. He was really young guy called Asif and I wasn't sure he knew how to drive our minibus, and I wasn't going to risk him with my lads. So we told Azeer to send him for a test and soon found out he couldn't reverse a car. He'd never had to in his village, so we couldn't use him. We sent for another which upset him no end. Mr. Belali was sympathetic but Mr. Rebdi wanted to send him home. I wanted to try him on something different. I always think it's best to solve something rather than dismiss it. So I proposed putting him on the small A4 scanner. Nick agreed and I asked Asif if he would consider it. He was unhappy with the idea that he might be sent home in disgrace, so said he'd have a go. It was the easiest job in the office and very monotonous, boring really, but he took to it and it just about suited his ability. So he kept his job and we had to promote Jojo so a win win after all.

The agreement for Donde arrived from Kuwait so he came home with us at the weekend to Bahrain with his girlfriend Lia. We had arranged a flight to Kuwait where someone would pick them up. They stayed a night with us and Kaitlin talked to Lia most of the evening, reassuring her it would be OK. She was a maid with a small family and she had been scared to leave because she thought they would get caught travelling together without being married. We got them on the flight the next day and sat back to wait for the aftershock. We went back to work after the weekend and carried on as if nothing had happened. It looked like we were getting a new centre forward.

***

Nick had been the main man at Aramco and I just went in as a support for the scanners and to check any configuration problems.

Aramco had so much data we had the idea of selling them a data package which we could tailor for them and administer. Then supply data entry staff, it seemed like a job for life. We'd done some research and found a company from Boston in the USA that did just what we needed. So one day we came up with a deal and approached Aramco with it. Too late: we'd missed the boat, they had just recently invested in a similar thing. We knew of it and were convinced it was the wrong one, ours was better. Anyway we went in and found the guy who was installing and configuring it. His name was Sean and he was Scottish so Nick got on with him straight away. When they got going I couldn't understand a word said between them. We saw him a few times but we knew it was hopeless to change their mind. We met Sean a few times after work and he became a really good friend.

We still liked our idea, though, and followed it up by booking a weeks' training for me in Boston in the New Year.

A Princely Visit

With all the new contacts we were definitely getting noticed and seemed to be out visiting most days, but one particular day we were told to make sure we were in the office and come wearing suits. Now this was unusual as we were normally left to make our own plans. Not on this occasion, because a member of the royal family was coming to the office. I knew we had been doing well and were getting noticed in high places but not that high. It was no other than Prince Turki Bin Mohammed Al Saud. I asked around and found out that his mother was Seeta bint Abdulaziz Al Saud and she was King Fahd's sister, so in my book that made him the king's nephew.

I remembered him from the first day of the first show before this all started. He looked about my age, but you can't tell with the dishdasha they wear, with Rayban sunglasses and a plain white headdress and rope. These were his working clothes.

His entourage consisted of around thirty advisers, so the conference room was packed and we needed to borrow some chairs from the main office. There were bodyguards in there as well, I'm sure. He stared at me as he came slowly into the room. He made me feel as if I wanted to apologise for something. I was thinking, what the hell is going on here?

After introductions, which took a while, we sent Azeer out for food. While we waited one of the advisors explained the prince wanted to buy Arabscan. What?!

First of all I was shocked both Rebdi and Belali were in at the same time, and also I was shocked that they both looked like they knew about this. Why wouldn't they know before me, idiot, they owned the place. They were smiling and, like everything we did, they expected me and Nick to make this work. Nick was asked to go through what we do and show our projected sales and stuff like that. We needed him to feel comfortable as we pushed him to make what we knew would be an uncomfortable decision. We had to exert authority while being aware of the power each of his advisers at the table wielded. We needed to convince his group of men who were in control of everything to join us.

I was being quiet in the corner, wondering if I was needed for this at all. I was actually trying to recover from shock that I was sitting in the same room as a member of the royal family. Can you imagine having a business meeting with the English royal family? At this time in my life, this was the closest I was likely to get to any royal family member anywhere.

My actual job was to gauge each reaction, to read the room quickly watching facial expressions, eye movements and body language and report after the meeting.

Azeer came back with pizza and burgers.

This was royalty, for Christ's sake, and he brought pizza and burgers, can you believe it?

The prince seemed at ease and liked the food and wanted anything he could get his hands on. I was thinking what a pig he was, he ate like one at least. He was not interested in the least at the discussions and carried on eating while his closest advisor Abdullah Mowabi carried on negotiating with Mr. Belali about the buyout. One guy was taking notes the whole time like a secretary but most of the prince's entourage had not so much as an inkling as to what we were talking about and were so bored, and a couple looked like they may fall asleep soon.

After the meeting broke, the note taker introduced himself as Salah Baban and promised us a copy of the minutes of the meeting. The prince suggested that Salah should make regular visits to us to check on our setup and report back. A bit more work for me to make a report for him each week. He said he was making a special trip down once a week from Riyadh to see us, but it seemed to me he was swinging the lead a bit and enjoying the day out.

We sat back to think where we were going from here.

'Go home and think about it,' said Mr. Belali.

'That's fine but I'm still buzzing inside,' I said.

'It's OK, we'll discuss it again tomorrow,' said Nick.

Chapter 11

Join Forces

Partners

When we got home Nick said we'd have dinner and go over the day's talks. He managed to speak calmly about the take-over and explain how it could be good or bad.

Then he brought up another 'Oh my God you're having a laugh' moment.

He calmly explained part of his contract said he would receive twenty five percent of any profit made by sales made after he joined, including company buyouts.

'What the! That's impressive, how did you manage that?' I asked him.

'It doesn't matter how, I'm offering you half, that's twelve and a half percent of all profits from now on,' he said.

I was not sure how to respond for a minute or two.

'Got any more Jack Daniels?' I asked. 'Let me get this straight, you're offering me a percentage of all sales that the company makes from now on including if the prince buys us?'

'That's right, half of my quarter of any profit,' he said.

As I said, an 'Oh my God' moment. I stood up and walked round the kitchen diner in a daze as it sank in. It was obviously a no brainer and by the time I'd done one a full circle I'd decided.

'Yes, I agree.' What else could I say, no?

We shook on it and out of the blue I was officially a shareholder in Arabscan.

This was not something to be taken lightly and I considered my position carefully. I still didn't trust an Arab, although these boys were a bit more secure than Saud Al Harbi.

Anyway, I stored it away in my brain for later. I hoped it came to good use one day.

Each day brought another adventure and this was no exception. I felt good being a new part percentage owner of Arabscan. Even if it was a secret deal.

Mike & Vien

We had bigger ambitions than most and wanted to be the best dealer in both bestselling software packages in our line of work but we needed technical support in both too. We'd heard an English guy giving a presentation of new computers in Bahrain who could give us an edge over our rivals and knew their products as well. There was another show coming up so we arranged to go. We found out his name was Mike and he lived in Bahrain, not far from us. Mike was a technical support engineer working for Silicon Graphics who knew nearly everything there was to know about the ins and outs of computing. I remember going to watch the show, and the images that were being shown blew my mind. They were showing some of the computerised effects used in the movie *The Day After Tomorrow*. I thought I was pretty good, but they made me realise how little I knew. During the after-show party we collared him and offered him a chance to join us.

He was intrigued and invited us to dinner at his home the following night to discuss a deal. His wife was from Thailand

and she made a meal for us. It was the first time I'd had cold-hot spicy food; it nearly blew my head off. I told him to look after her, she was a bargain.

He asked us to confirm it was a family deal and that his son Richard could go to the British School before he would commit. Also, the money had better be good, as his wife Vien wouldn't be allowed to work in Saudi without a sponsor.

Bahrain laws were slightly different to Saudi laws because you were allowed to give notice and leave any time during your contract if you wanted, whereas in Saudi you had to work the length of the contract before leaving. It would mean he would have to live in Al-Khobar, but he would get a new house on a smart compound as opposed a small bungalow in downtown Manama.

He agreed to join us and we became friends, so much so that when I eventually finished my time in Saudi and came home he followed me and came to work for me. I sponsored Vien and his son Richard to live in England.

Mike had lived in the Middle East for around ten years, which meant he knew nearly every haunt and diamond food outlet, dodgy or not. I was soon eating in all the best burger joints in Bahrain. I'd never heard of 'Fuddruckers' before but I assure you it was the best burger I'd ever had then or since. Or Schlotzsky's for open pastrami sandwiches with pickles on sourdough bread.

The middle east trade show was coming up in Dubai again and we were invited to be the Saudi Arabian representatives for both of the biggest software companies in the world because of our dealerships. I would be on one stand and Mike would be on the other.

I asked for a week's break before the show to see my family. They came for a week during school half term.

Our villa had four bedrooms so the three children could share a room. It was massive anyway compared to their bedrooms in the UK. When they arrived, my wife couldn't believe the place. To her I was living in luxury while she was bringing up our children by herself in our end of terrace house in south Croydon. What am I supposed to do about that? I'm committed to sharing with Nick and Kaitlin for a year.

On the first night of their visit the children played in the pool while the adults sat by and enjoyed a drink. The evening temperature was pretty perfect and quite a lot higher than England. Nick was showing off a bit and managed to throw both my sons in the pool, and me as well, come to think of it. He just pushed me and the chair I was sitting in straight over the edge. I was fully clothed and sank like a stone. I came up like I'd swallowed the whole pool.

During the week my fifteen year old daughter wanted to walk around in a bathing costume or shorts, so I had to explain that was OK inside the compound but not advisable outside or in town, or even this country for that matter.

'I'm on holiday and I'm hot and its lovely here,' was her answer.

'I know that,' I said. 'It's OK in the compound but in town the men are going to stare at you dressed like that and you won't like it.'

I got it all wrong and instead of making sure she covered up a bit more, I let her, and she got the shock of her life in the market. Men were going round holding hands and gawking at her. Some came around for a second look. We went to the country club to get away from the locals and relax in their garden bar. Still, the damage was done and she was so upset she couldn't enjoy the day. My eldest son asked why the men were holding hands.

'They are brothers or cousins who are here working away from their own country like me,' I told him.

'It looks a bit weird,' he said.

We went to Shaikh's beach and it was idyllic, a bit like paradise. A beautiful warm breeze, swaying palm trees, soft white sand and a lawn like a Wimbledon tennis court. The water was so shallow I could walk out with my youngest son on my shoulders for about a hundred yards.

***

After my family left I went with Mike to Dubai for the trade show. Hamad had arranged an apartment close to the business area. Dubai is split into districts, like business, technology and gold souk. We had a rental car and made our own way to and from the show each day. Mike was suffering from diabetes and he had to inject insulin each morning before we left the apartment. It meant he couldn't drink much alcohol, or anything really, but he hadn't been to the Emirates for a few years so one night he drank too much and the next day I couldn't rouse him. I started to panic and wasn't too sure what to do. I called Nick who called a doctor. I had to wait until he arrived, and I prayed he would be able to wake Mike and sort out the problem. He told me to go to the show and tell them Mike wouldn't be there today but he should be OK tomorrow. Everyone I told understood and told me not to worry. When I arrived back that evening Mike was watching television and said he was OK, but sorry for alarming me. Alarming me? I thought he was dead! Nick called and I told him Mike was OK and would be at the show the next day. He said the owners wanted to see Mike when he got back, as this might affect his insurance package they had arranged for him. Another thing I wasn't aware of was dealing with any kind of incurable sickness.

At least the trade show was another great success and we managed to drum up a ton of new leads.

***

There's an American airbase in Dhahran not far from the coast. They flew regularly over us and around the Kuwait border and the Persian Gulf. The Fahd military hospital is on the base.

Salah suggested we should call them. Mr. Rebdi asked me to arrange a visit. So I did and they asked if I could come and have a look at their historical documents and try to digitise them; I arranged to visit the next day. Security was very tight and there were military personnel all around, men and women. When we arrived they wanted our ID and reasons for the visit. Salah Baban was from Iraq but the prince had arranged a Saudi passport for him so he could move around easily. Not so easy to get into an American base, though. Quite a bit of checking took place before we could get in.

The head of records said they were thinking of transferring all their patient files onto computer. We asked to see the filing system and were led down a couple of staircases into a basement room that was damp and smelly with no natural light. The files were so old they went back decades and some were in a terrible condition, wet, torn with rodent-eaten corners. While we were making notes a security guard came and asked us to leave and re-schedule our visit for another day. He explained that an incident had occurred and everyone was being evacuated from the building. As we were leaving, Salah asked our guide what had happened and all he said was a nurse had been found dead. Jesus! Back at the office we spoke to Mr. Belali about it and he promised to find out more information and see if he could get us back in there as soon as possible; he definitely wanted this contract. He had a few friends in high places and after a couple of days he told us we wouldn't be going back for a few weeks, as the nurse had actually been murdered. It made the international press so we found out more by the end of the week. An Australian nurse had allegedly been murdered and the two British nurses had been accused and arrested. We'd only stumbled into a murder scene and not realized it. I knew we wouldn't get back in there until after Christmas so we tried to shut it out. I was planning to go home anyway, but we were still curious and read the papers for a few weeks until the story died away.

I had told everyone at home I would be back for Christmas and this gave me an incentive to make the days pass as quickly as possible. I began looking at flight times and got a buzz arranging my trip. All the airlines were offering discounts to try and get your business. I was glad I wasn't flying Saudi national airlines, though, as about a month before my flight a Saudia Boeing 747 collided with a Kazakhstan Airlines 11-76, costing the lives of 349 people. Good old British Airways is what I say.

***

I was daydreaming one day in the office, thinking about presents for my children, when there was a knock on my door.

'Can I see you for a minute, Mr. Dennis?' It was Asif, our young driver-come-scanner operator.

'Please come in and take a seat, how are you doing, is everything OK?' I asked him.

'Nothing wrong, sir, I just wanted to ask for a pay increase?' he asked. I was flabbergasted.

'Well, I don't know about that; where has this come from? I thought you were happy, Asif,' I replied.

He's nodding or shaking his head, I can't tell; what is it with all the nodding from the Indians?

'Can you stop shaking your head, I don't know if you're agreeing with me or not,' I said.

'I am happy sir, but I think I deserve a pay rise, see when I came I was a driver, and now I've been promoted to office worker and very important job of scanner operator as well,' he explained.

'I don't think so Asif, you were lucky to keep your job. Mr. Rebdi wanted to send you back home in disgrace,' I said. 'We have appraisals in the summer and I'll give you what I think you're worth after you've been here a year like everyone else, OK?' I told him and sent him packing.

Working for Arabscan was so different from working for myself. At Christmas I went home for a couple of weeks and really enjoyed it as I hadn't seen the family for a while. It was great to catch up and we had so much more to talk about than usual. It felt like real time off.

Three Weekends

When I arrived back at the office Mr. Belali called me into his office to tell me a few things. Small talk at first: he asked about my holiday and how were the family, then he told me I had taken too much time off and they would be docking me a couple of days' pay.

'How did I take too much?' I asked him. 'I left here on the Wednesday after work and returned on the Saturday two weeks later'

'I know,' he said, 'but you took three weekends.'

'Well, yes, three weekends but two weeks' vacation,' I said.

'I know that as well, but technically you should have returned on the Wednesday that is two weeks away,' he reasoned.

'But I'm not due back until today,' I said.

'Again, this is true, but we are being very reasonable allowing you to live in Bahrain,' he said. 'If you lived here we would have expected you to have returned two days ago.'

'But I always have Thursday and Friday off,' I said.

'Yes, but you are on call every day while you work for us,' he said. 'Just because you are living in another country you still officially work here, and we might need you at any time night or day,' he said.

'Well, that's news to me. It's never been explained to me that way before,' I said. 'I'll make a mental note to always be ready for a callout.'

He had to be joking. It's normal where I come from to leave on the Friday and return on the Monday, whether there is a week or two in between. Oh well, live and learn, I should have checked before making arrangements I suppose, but you can't know every rule in their book, I reckon they make it up as they go along.

Secondly, Prince Turki's man Salah Baban would be helping us a bit more. We were all to treat him with the same respect we would show the prince. He would help with some of the high profile companies and go on sales trips with Nick and me if we needed support. Great, I thought, he's spying on us and reporting back to the prince to see if we're any good and the company is worth purchasing.

Thirdly, the two British nurses had been found guilty and were in prison, and finally that trip we were hoping would happen was happening and I was off to Boston in the USA to get some more training. The good news was I'd be away for a week of Ramadan, which was great for me. The bad news was I was getting accustomed to thirty degrees during the day and twenty at night, whilst in Boston, it's zero and less at night. I was acclimatised to the heat now and didn't have any winter clothes. Also, you can't buy any in Bahrain or Al-Khobar; there's no need. I ended up borrowing a jacket from Nick. It would have to do, but I still nearly froze to death. The trip was organised by Hamid and because it was short notice I was in business class; my God, what a difference from economy seating.

I was going with Scottish Angus, a friend of John's who worked for a data management company. He had to keep that to himself as we were going to their main rival. Sean had finished his work at Aramco and had returned to the UK. Scottish Angus liked a drink so I had to be careful because I was a lightweight compared to him and Nick. The flight was the best I'd had in my life; I wanted to go business from then on. It was on Emirates Air straight to Heathrow, then change onto British Airways to New York. Then it got tricky; we needed to catch a prop plane up to Boston. What a come down, it only had a dozen seats. Hamid, what had you done? You went from one extreme to the next.

Still, the training went OK, it was the weather I was struggling with. Angus was all togged up and used to the cold, coming from the tip of the Scottish highlands. I was surprised he wasn't in a kilt with no underwear.

One night we ventured out for a drink and it was snowing and I couldn't feel my fingers or toes. The bar was warm, though, and it had sport on TV. Although the beer was all lager; it was the only thing that was good cold.

When we'd finished training, Angus was staying on a bit so I was going back on my own. I was all packed, not much, just a carry-on bag, so after checking out we went into town for a look around before I needed to go to the airport.

Boston is a great city and the Celtics played there so Angus was happy. It was mainly populated by the Irish so there were plenty of bars and pubs. After finding the smallest Irish bar in the world, they say – it's just wider than the width of the door – we both had a pint of Guinness and Angus wanted whiskey chasers.

'OK for you,' I said, 'you're not flying today, I'll just have the one.'

That prop plane was on my mind and it was a real prop job.

So it was back to New York. The plane wasn't full and they were asking people to move seats to manage the trim. I ask you. There were some humungous people on board, mind you.

The turbulence was terrible as we didn't fly at a great height so I almost threw up. I told you I was a bit lightweight in the drinking department. But I was looking forward to spending the night in New York.

New York, New York; I was so glad to get off that so called jet I was now on cloud nine.

I was queuing for a cab next to a tall thin man with a ten gallon hat who looked like Clint Eastwood and he asked, in a Texan drawl, where I was staying.

'I'm in the Marriott on Lexington Avenue,' I replied.

'So am I, do you want to share the cab?' he asked.

I thanked him and we shared the next cab and chatted all the way.

When we arrived he wouldn't let me pay and we both went to check in. He was first and had an argument about the size of his room. He was a very tall guy, and I assume he'd reserved a giant size bed.

I was next, but when I got to the desk I couldn't find my wallet. It wasn't in any of my pockets or my bag. Now what was I going to do? I had some cash in my pocket but not enough for the night. The checking in clerk was very helpful she asked me where I'd last used it and what cards were in it. I told her I had it at the airport because I'd changed some money into dollars and that I had an American Express card. She told me to keep the cash and she'd call American Express for me. They were brilliant and after some personal questions they agreed to pay for my night and bill me. She also called the door man and ordered a cab to take me back to the airport to look for my wallet; the driver waited for me while I searched for it. No sign of it at the airport, the bureau de change hadn't seen it and nobody had handed one in. He took me back to the hotel and then charged me $70 for the ride. Now I was in New York on a Saturday night, miserable and almost broke. It was late so I decided to go to bed and I'd sort out something in the morning, God knows what though.

I was almost asleep when the phone rang. It was strange to get a call now, so I thought it was reception.

'Is that Mr. Norman?'

'Yes, who's calling?'

'It's the concierge from the Intercontinental Barclay hotel across the street from the Marriott and I've got your wallet.'

I keep saying this but I couldn't believe it. Another 'Oh my God' moment springs to mind.

'You are a life saver, thank you, I'll be right across to get it.'

I dressed quickly and rushed out to find him. As I got to the door of the Barclay, the doorman is telling someone about some guy who's lost his wallet.

'That's me,' I said.

I asked for the concierge at the desk.

'Someone handed it in, you must have dropped it in the street,' he said.

'How did you find me?' I asked.

'I looked through it and called American Express who told me your story, then I called the Marriott and they found you for me.'

'Thanks again. I can't believe it, it's a minor miracle,' I said.

I went back across the street to my hotel and straight to reception where I told them I'd got my wallet back and how.

'I suggest you buy a lottery ticket, sir, you're the luckiest man in New York tonight,' said the desk clerk.

'I'm heading for the bar first,' I decided.

So I'd missed the best of the New York evening, but I could still get a drink and buy breakfast and afford to get the airport in the morning. Trouble was, all my cards were cancelled, but I still had some Saudi money in the wallet.

When I woke up the next morning there was a fast check out bill on the mat by the door. American Express had paid the bill and I'd been checked out, so breakfast was going to have to be a diner.

First I needed to change some riyals for dollars.

It's not so easy on a Sunday morning in Manhattan. After walking the streets for what seemed like an hour trying hotel receptions and bureaux de change, I eventually found a place on Madison Avenue. Armed with some dollars I attacked my breakfast with gusto.

'Goodbye New York, I'll be back,' I shouted.

The flight was by Gulf Air via Geneva but at least it was business class, and I was absolutely knackered so used the little blindfold they give you in a pouch and slept most of the way, until I was rudely woken up during the stopover in Geneva by the cleaners vacuuming the plane. Half the passengers in economy got off and a new crowd arrived. I was getting to be a real snob these days.

When I eventually got back Ramadan, the fasting month, was finished and it was Eid-al-Fitr; there's seven days of feasting. Although I'd never seen any fasting, only gorging after sundown. So no work for three days as the whole Muslim community was celebrating the new moon. Relaxing and enjoying the time off by the pool, how the other half live eh!

Two Shaikhs

Back to work and we were asked to attend a meeting with one of Mr. Belali's old school friends, Shaikh Khalifa Al Khalifa. The Shaikh was a Bahraini and the manager of the causeway bridge between Saudi and Bahrain. The Bahrainis only allowed the bridge to be built if they could manage it. They maintained that they didn't want to go to Saudi, but the Saudis wanted to come to Bahrain. The causeway always needed some repair work and Mr. Belali had entrusted us with this particular task. Shaikh Al Khalifa had been friends with Mr. Belali for forty years and he knew Arabscan were one of the best companies to do this. We met him and his nephew Shaikh Hmood Al Khalifa and they decided we were well equipped to do the work. So we were going to prepare some new plans and sub-contract the building work out.

I let Nick talk business with Shaikh Khalifa and I chatted with Shaikh Hmood about Bahrain. We became friendly and he gave me his business card, which I always carried because you never know when you might need a friend. My stack of cards was getting higher.

Kaitlin's Gardener

Kaitlin loved her garden and even though it was mostly sand, she wanted flowers and plants to brighten up the place. Our villa had a fabulous entrance hall. All tiled walls and stone flooring; we even had a low wall separating the lounge area from the hallway. This was made up of double brickwork and was crying out for some plants. The compound employed some Pakistani gardeners to tend the communal areas that we all shared. One day Kaitlin asked one young lad to come in and plant something in the spaces between the low walls. The gardener was thrilled with the invitation and came to have a look at where she wanted them so he could arrange for them.

He told her he would order them the next day and they should be here in a couple of days. He came back after the weekend to plant them. They looked very nice to me when I came home that evening. The next day he didn't arrive to finish the planting, so Kaitlin asked around to find out why.

It turned out he had been beaten so badly he couldn't go to work that day or any day for a week. When Nick asked the lead gardener about it, he was told the other gardeners thought he had been intimate with Kaitlin and they resented it. The culture problem arises again.

Chapter 12

Aramco

Oil and sand

Our main contract was with a company called Aramco, the largest oil and gas company in Saudi Arabia.

Large oil reserves were first identified in the Dhahran area in 1931, and in 1935, Standard Oil drilled the first commercially viable oil well. Standard Oil later established a subsidiary in Saudi Arabia called the Arabian American Oil Company (ARAMCO), now fully owned by the Saudi government and known as Saudi Aramco. Dhahran has been the home of Saudi Aramco's headquarters for 80 years and is its first and largest gated compound with more than 9,700 residents. Employees and dependents of Aramco, known as Aramcons, have a tendency to use Dhahran to solely refer to the Aramco camp while using Al-Khobar and/or Dammam to refer to the area outside the camp. The Saudi Aramco Residential Camp makes up much of the city of Dhahran.

***

We had arranged for us to transfer all their seismic plans to computerised documents.

No company had been able to do this before because they were so wide and long they needed a Scangraphics machine, another clever idea from Nick.

I'd had my training in America but we needed one or two of the big ones I'd been trained on. We persuaded Mr. Belali to buy one from each of the companies I'd visited so we could rent one to Aramco and put some of our guys in their office to use it.

When the first one arrived from Scangraphics, it was listed in the delivery manifest as a scanner. The customs thought it was a human body scanner and held it at the customs depot.

We had what we called a 'gopher' whose name was Azeer, and like Mosem, he used to sort out any problems we had with the authorities. He told us they wouldn't release it until we had opened it and proved it was harmless. It was in a massive packing case and we needed a small crane to lift it. We hired one and a flatbed truck to move it. When we eventually opened it the customs guys all stood around looking at it and scratching their heads

'What ees it?' one guy said. 'Where do the people go?'

'It's not for people, it's a paper scanner, and be careful 'cos it's got five cameras inside it and they are all configured,' I shouted.

'Calm down and don't call him an idiot,' Azeer whispered to me.

'Well, tell them not to drop it,' I said.

'If they drop it we're stuffed, we'll never get another,' said Nick.

So we try to pack it back up without much success and load it on the flatbed truck.

When we arrived at Aramco, the main gate wouldn't let us in without a letter from head office, so we turned round and took it back to our office.

'We'll have to leave it in the underground car park for tonight,' said Azeer. 'It's too big and there's nowhere else. I'll cover it over with a tarpaulin so at least it's undercover.'

The following day we had the right paperwork and got through the gate at last. When we got to the main building we called ahead and asked for a trolley. There was no way anybody could carry it.

It filled the lift and it was a nightmare trying to get it round the corners to the small office they had allocated us.

It took us all morning, but eventually we had it in place. Then I had to do a test and see if the cameras had moved. Of course, they had; it was just my luck, so I took the front off and adjusted the cameras surrounded by a group of Aramco engineers.

I'd picked three teams of four to do eight hour shifts, but it wasn't easy getting them to and fro. We only had one driver so he had to work three shifts in a single day. Also, guys were arriving home in the middle of the night and trying to sleep when others were leaving for the main office in the morning. There is a hand over period as well for each shift.

The Boys were asleep

I visited Aramco three times a week to see how my men were getting on and check the time cards and meet with the Aramco engineers. This was mostly in the daytime, and ninety percent of the time it was alright.

Although once thought I would try and catch them out, and I went in the middle of the night and a couple were asleep. I left them there and went to find some coffee, which would keep me awake more; I knew there was always some brewing in the nearby breakout area. I sat for ten minutes drinking and thinking it through. I went back to the office and one had woken up. I thought the others would wake them, but one guy was out of it. The other one was distraught for getting caught and pleaded with me not to punish him. I gave him the benefit of the doubt but told the others to wake their mate up and I would be talking to them all the following day. I was sure they took it in turns to get a nap during the shift. I needed to work out a way to keep their spirits up and save them losing face with their friends.

Another day I popped in for a chat before the weekly meeting and was informed they had lost some files from the computer. I didn't have a lot of time to help find them and went straight to the meeting room to be confronted with a young Aramco engineer accusing us of negligence, and saying we were irresponsible and should be removed from the project.

'Wait a minute,' I said. 'I've only just been informed of this and I need to ascertain the degree of the problem.'

'You've been slack and we can't afford to lose important information,' he said.

'I'm sure we can rectify the situation, let me go and find out more,' I asked.

He was adamant we should be removed from the job. I thought, he's jumping the gun a bit here; I didn't even know the state of things.

I went to our office and asked Michael, who was in charge of the shift that day, what happened and how bad it was.

'We copied some files the wrong way between two folders is all,' he admitted. 'It's not a big thing, we can get them back.'

'We still have the back-up disks don't we?' I asked.

'Yes, it won't take long, about an hour.'

I went back to find the pompous engineer, young upstart, I was thinking. He had already told his boss and I had to find him and explain our mistake and how we would correct it. When I found him I was furious; I told myself to calm down and explain.

'Tell your young engineer he can't go off half-cocked before he has all the facts. He could affect people's lives and we all have families to look after. If we get kicked off this project it will affect Arabscan's reputation and their future work with Aramco,' I said.

'This is a complex thing my team are doing and sometimes human error comes into it. That's the reason we have back-ups. I'm sure that by the time we finish talking it will be back to normal,' I explained. He told me to go and correct the problem and tell him when it was done.

I went and told Michael to restore the backup and I went for some lunch. I returned after lunch and the files had been restored and we had lost about two hours of work, so not the end of the world. Michael knew they would have to work a bit harder to get back on time, but he was prepared for it. I thanked him for fixing it so quickly and the rest of the lads for backing him up. I always tried to encourage them because I too needed reassurance.

I went back and found the chief engineer and told him where we were and he relented and said carry on. He was grateful for us telling him and not covering up our mistake.

Honesty is still the best policy.

***

We had a few Aramco site offices with teams of guys living and working away together. One was in Abqaiq, which I called 'Ab Cake', and on one of my site visits I went there to visit the boys and got stopped by the police. I didn't know what had happened at first, because it is a straight stretch of road through what seemed like a desert and probably was. I was flagged down by a police car and told to pull over by the side of the road. Three other cars were there and two police land cruisers. I was a bit bewildered and asked what was happening. The policeman answered me in Arabic and I obviously couldn't understand him. I was looking around for help when one of the other drivers came over, who was American, and told me I'd been caught speeding. Well I never, I thought, it's a long straight road with hardly any traffic on it just like a motorway back in England. I didn't even know there was a speed limit. It was a bit ironic because I'd been listening to the track by America called 'A Horse With No Name.'

Have a listen to it sometime and you'll appreciate what I mean. Anyway, I needed to sign a form but it was all in Arabic and I was not sure what I was signing.

'You have to sign it or they'll take you in,' the Yank said. 'That is not a good idea. It'll be OK, your company will sort it out back at the office, just hand it in and they'll pay the fine too.'

I took it back and gave it to Hamid, who went ape and told me off. He called Mr. Rebdi, who was in, and he told Azeer to go and pay the fine.

'I've been stopped nearly every time I've been on that road,' he said.

I couldn't go back to Bahrain that night because all fines had to be paid in full before you could leave the Kingdom. So Hamid arranged for me to stay in a hotel that night.

One day I visited my team in the Aramco offices. They were all OK and my meeting went OK. On my way out, I was stopped at the gate and asked to come to the office. I parked and went in and was immediately shown a form and asked to sign it. I couldn't read it as it was in Arabic, so I refused. The guard called someone and I was shown into a room with a chair and asked to wait for an interpreter. Once he arrived he explained it had shown up on their CCTV cameras that I had been without my seat belt. A seat belt? Nobody wears a seat belt in Saudi. Well they do in Aramco, as I found out to my cost. I'd been tuning the radio and not even thought about fastening it. Aramco had their own radio station and it played country music 24/7, which used to wind me up. This was a big problem for me, because it was considered rude. Mr. Belali told me to write a letter of apology to the head guy in Aramco or I wouldn't be allowed to visit their offices again. Not only that, it had embarrassed Arabscan.

I got another slapped wrist from Mr. Belali.

We'd heard from the Kuwait office that Donde had been on vacation and had decided not to return, so we were in a bit of a fix for technical support. He had manipulated us and we'd helped him get out before his contract was up.

We never saw Donde or Lia ever again.

***

Nick was always messing around and one evening when the Bahraini customs office asked if we had anything to declare, he said, 'Him,' pointing to me. The shock on my face showed, so the guy asked to pat me down. Now there's a joke and a joke, but I didn't think it was me until that day. I could have been arrested as a terrorist. Can you believe it, in the Middle East I was being accused of smuggling?

We left the office one weekend to go home, it was my turn to drive and we were expecting the usual casual escape. Instead there was a problem at customs; the computers had gone down on the Saudi side and everyone was getting a going over using manpower instead. The holdup caused a tailback nearly all the way back to Saudi and the traffic moved in fits and starts. We couldn't move in the pandemonium, but in the searing heat we needed the air conditioning on in the car and therefore we kept the engine running. We boiled over just as we arrived at the customs toll gates. We needed help, but the customs guys were all too busy keeping the drivers from rioting; horns were blasting by angry men. Our car was had an automatic gearbox so we couldn't even bump start it, so in the end we suggested leaving it and getting a cab. Not a good idea, as we were told any cars left overnight in the customs area would be classed as a threat and destroyed. They made us wait hours until the queue died down and then got us going; I think they were glad to be rid of us actually. When we finally arrived home we headed for the drinks cabinet. That was the first but not the last time we needed a drink after the journey.

***

You can't get pork, bacon or ham in Saudi but you can in Bahrain. So on occasion Nick and I used to buy it in Spinney's supermarket and take it in to the office for the lads. The guys working in Spinney's asked if we were taking it over and if we were, they would repack it and label it as veal so we wouldn't get stopped at customs. Nick used to call out when we arrived, 'Who wants a bacon sandwich today then?' This would get a big cheer from the non-Muslim boys.

We were relaxing at home one weekend when we got a call from the main gate. Mr. Rebdi had driven over to visit us and wanted to come in for a 'cup of tea' he said, and to see where we had chosen to live. Between us we managed to drink a bottle of Jack Daniels during the afternoon. He was so out of it we had to book him into a local aparthotel called Mansouri Mansions in Manama for the night. There was no way he could drive back to Saudi.

Now I knew why Bahrain was called 'the bar at the end of the road' for Saudis.

Desert Roses

I had a couple of mates working in Qatar, George and John. I'd worked with both at various times about fifteen and ten years ago respectively. John had worked in Abu Dhabi for a year at one of the companies I'd visited with Ron a few years before. They both worked for an oil company and had their wives with them. John called me and asked for a demonstration of my products. I put it to Nick and he agreed it was a good idea. So I arranged a trip to his office. John told me to make sure I had two hundred Qatari riyals inside my passport, to speed up customs, he said. I flew to Doha and explained to the customs guy who I was visiting and lied about the reason, telling him I was just visiting for a few days. I'd arranged the trip for a Wednesday so I could stay until Friday evening before coming back.

It was another palaver as I had to go to another building and get a special import stamp. There was a queue and I was the only person who couldn't speak the lingo. I was sent from pillar to post for a bit then eventually got an entry stamp. I was getting used to Middle East taxi cabs by now and had the full address and phone number with me. No problems this time, we went straight there, although it was in the middle of town on the main street. John welcomed me and showed me round the office and I saw George as well. In the evenings I was to stay at George's apartment, which was massive and on the top floor of a block overlooking most of the city. George's wife Amanda had arranged a couple of quiz nights and tonight was the first. When she came in she asked if I would mind going to John's that evening for dinner, as they had a few people coming over for the quiz and dinner. I wasn't bothered, just a bit confused, until she explained it would be the same quiz for both nights but a different crowd the following night. I understood now, as I would know the answers for the following night. I went to John's and had a fantastic meal with his wife Linda and their son Rob. Then back to George's to sleep. The following day was Thursday and John suggested we join a group that was driving out into the desert for some dune fun and bar-b-queuing on the beach. 'Great fun,' he said.

John had a Grand Cherokee Jeep which we could all fit in easily. We drove off road and ended up exploring the sand dunes near the water's edge by the inland sea. It's said you can see Saudi Arabia on a clear day, which is every day. If you dig down in the sand a few feet you can find desert roses, fossilised sand which resembles a rose. They are quite unique and apparently you are not allowed to take them out of the country, so they check your luggage at customs.

On the way back I was sure the lead driver took a wrong turn, I don't know how because there were no roads. Anyway, the convoy had to stop and we all got out. The drivers had a chat and we all got back in turned around and went back a couple of miles until another car took over at the front and found our way back to the main road. As far as I was concerned I was completely lost; everywhere I looked was sand, it was really hot and no sign of a road.

When we arrived back at John's place he said, 'Next time you come we'll go to the 42km beach, it's called that because there's only one road sign as you leave town, so you have to set your trip meter to zero when you see it, and when you've driven 42km turn right and carry on until you get to the sea. It's the most beautiful place on earth.'

The quiz night was a laugh and we all went out to dinner, which was a midnight feast in a small restaurant with outside tables under the stars.

Friday was the most fun day because George took me to his golf club. Golf club, I hear you say, in the desert? Yes, in fact, it's a bit classy and only expats are allowed in. There were mostly Scandinavian and American members but George was the token Brit. The company they worked for was Danish and the staff all came from there. The course was sand, obviously, and the greens are brown; they are raised and soaked in oil to stop the sand from blowing around in the wind. I borrowed some clubs from George. He was reluctant to lend me his best ones so he found me three from the club changing room cupboard, a driver, a five iron, and a putter. I'd only played golf a few times in my life so I tried out with a bucket of balls on the driving range first. I was not bad, at least I could hit the damn things. Anyway as we went for the round and as I was about to take my first tee shot, I asked George to photograph me striking the ball. After my shot I looked at George and his jaw is almost on the ground.

'What's the matter, I thought it was a good shot?'

'You said you'd never been any good at this.'

'I'm not.'

'Well, that was a fantastic tee shot, better than some for their first shot.'

'Get out of it, let me see the picture.'

'I didn't take it, I was so shocked with what I witnessed I forgot.'

'Oh thanks, now no one will believe me.'

'You'll know.'

Well, that's as good as it got, and I finished the round about fifteen over par. The fairways were firm sand and the ball bounced, but not very far, then rolled so you could follow the line of the ball in the sand, but the rough was just a load of small rocks. If you hit the rough you could kiss your ball goodbye as it bounced any way you can imagine. Everyone carried a small square piece of fake turf with them, and they used it on the fairways for their second or third shots. The greens, or browns as they were called, were packed solid and were completely flat. You had to chip up onto them but when the ball landed and ran it left a small groove and you could see the line. It made putting easier. There were no bunkers as such, just soft sand on either side of the browns. My bunker shots just went straight over to the one on the other side; I blamed it on George for not getting me a pitching wedge, but really my touch was terrible. Still, I had a great weekend with friends and it was a much needed break from the norm and some beer after the round.

When I was leaving, George said he'd be coming to Bahrain in a few months as his visa was running out and he needed to leave Qatar for the weekend. He explained his British passport allowed him to stay for three months and then he had to leave for a couple of days and get a new stamp each time he returned. Apparently everyone was doing it and it saved the company money not having to register everyone who they employed. I liked that idea and wished the Saudis trusted people like the Qataris did. So I went back to Saudi and thought about my own vacation.

The next weekend we Nick got a call from Neil and Simon. They wanted to stay with us for a day before flying to England for a break. It wasn't a problem so they came across the bridge with us. Neil brought his girlfriend Michel with him and along the way they explained they needed to get out of Saudi, as someone had informed on them about their bar. The religious police were on the warpath and anyone found with alcohol would be in big trouble. As they worked for British Aerospace they couldn't afford to be found out. The company had told them to have a month off to allow the problem to die down. They would go and keep checking when to come back.

Two Easters

Nick dropped a bombshell on me one weekend. He had been meeting Owen, the Bentley rep, in secret. Owen had told him he had had enough of the Middle East job and was returning to Wales at Easter. He had been authorised to offer Nick his job and he was thinking about it. Oh my God where would that leave me? I dreaded to think. I was glad I was going home soon too, to think about it.

It was in my contract that I could have two paid trips home per year and I'd chosen Christmas and Easter. So I took the first couple of weeks and flew home. I visited my parents as it was my dad's birthday a week after Good Friday. He didn't look too good but mum said she was looking after him and he'd be fine.

She called me on Easter Monday as he'd fallen out of bed. I rushed over and when I arrived he was on the floor wedged beside the bed and the bedside cupboard. I tried to pick him up but couldn't; he was a dead weight. Mum was panicking and just wanted me to get him back into bed and she would look after him. I argued and ended up calling the doctor and ambulance. The doctor turned up and went ballistic. It turned out he'd had a stroke. Mum was in a bad way, almost fainting, so I went with him to the hospital. I visited him every day that week and was with him on his sixty fourth birthday on the Friday. I wanted to stay more but I had a flight to catch and in the end I had to get back to work.

It was a crap holiday but I'm glad I was there to help in the end. I didn't know then that would be the last day I would ever see him.

When I got back it was Eid-al-Adha, a public holiday, so the whole country grinds to a halt for three days. The rich Saudi boys go out in their yellow Ford Mustangs and drive round like lunatics. So it was like I got two Easter breaks this year, one at home and one at work.

***

My first day back and I received a message saying there had been a fire at the Hajj and we were on tenterhooks waiting for news of our lads. Nick had moved some of the lads around to cover for them while I'd been away so I didn't know much about it but it had caused some disruption. Some of the Christian lads were always complaining they had to cover for the Muslims when they were away. A couple of days later we got the news we had been dreading: we had lost two lads, Satish and Preeth, at the camping site. This stopped everything and brought it all into perspective, as we should have been respecting their pilgrimage and not been bickering about a few more hours' work. I knew a bit about grief as I'd lost relatives recently, and it's reported there are eight signs of grief: denial, anger, bargaining, guilt, depression, loneliness, acceptance and hope. Most of my team suffered some form of grief for their friends and my door was open for them to air their feelings. When you look after young people away from their families, there are times when you have to be a psychologist as well.

Chapter 13

All Over the Place

Into the frying pan

Nick had been trying to get Mr. Rebdi to pay him his part of the profits as his contract stated. He was adamant that his contract had a clause stating he was entitled to twenty five percent of all profits made from sales made by him. It was Mr. Belali who pointed out it was only due once he'd completed his contract.

Saudi contracts came with a bonus scheme to help when the contract ended. If you completed two years, you would receive two weeks' pay when you left. As he was only in the middle of his first year, he had to let that go as well. He was becoming frustrated and had to let Bentley know his decision; they wanted someone with knowledge of the area. The deal they offered him was fifty percent better, so he accepted.

Mr. Belali and Mr. Rebdi both wanted him to stay, so they offered him a pay rise, which wasn't enough. So when he offered his resignation they would only agree if he relinquished his percentage deal. He wanted out so he let it go and I lost my bit as well. All the major deals were still in progress except the Prince Turki one. He'd come to see us once a month for about six months, but I think he got bored of it all and returned to Riyadh to spend his money on something a bit more interesting and profitable.

I still lived with Nick and Kaitlin because of the year's lease, but Mr. Belali asked him to repay his bit for the remaining time. In the meantime, Kaitlin went out and got a couple of golden Labrador puppies and I went looking for another place to live. She said she fell in love with one puppy and couldn't bear to separate him from the last one of the litter. They were put in the utility room at night and they howled for most of it. The utility room was right behind my bedroom, so I could hear them and they kept me awake most nights.

Shaikh Hmood offered me a villa on one of his compounds and I went with Nick to visit it, but it was a too big and I would rattle around in it feeling lost again like Egyptian village. I saw a few apartments around town but eventually I stayed.

Nick left Arabscan and I was put in temporary charge.

Holding the Baby

Things were going well for Nick in his new job. Kaitlin had given birth to a son and Nick was obviously very pleased with himself because he went out and bought an open top MG. It didn't have air conditioning, though, so it must have been a nightmare to drive out there.

Suddenly Kaitlin had another mouth to feed and she had good days and bad days. Really happy one minute and sad the next. To say the least, we fell out, and Kaitlin wanted a bit more from me towards the day to day running of the villa. I explained I'd used all my accommodation money towards the rent and was sending virtually all the rest home, so I had barely enough to keep me going each month. She said they were paying for most of the food and I had to pay more. I said

I'd move out, but Nick explained to her that if I left they would not be able to stay because he'd have to pay my contribution towards the rent. So, we agreed to disagree and I went out for McDonald's or curry for my food from then on. Cheeseburgers sitting in the car looking at the sea, comfort food. Thank god for vitamin pills and oranges or I would have had scurvy.

***

I went out by myself for the evening to the 'Red House Bar', a bar diner on the way to Manama. I had some food and sat at the bar nursing a drink and thinking about how to tackle the job coming at me when Keith came in. I explained what had happened and we chatted for a while. Keith wasn't there to talk to me, though.

They always had some live music and this night Keith was joining them. At first it sounded like an irritable group of musicians trying to tune their instruments but couldn't decide who had the wrong key, but they soon found their rhythm and it was rather good. Keith played lead guitar and sang on the Eagles hit 'Hotel California' and it was wonderful. It was a real jam night and guys were arriving and adding to the group for one number, then sitting at the bar waiting for some tune they knew then they would go and play. One bloke arrived and played the drums for one song and then left. All together a great night and one I wasn't expecting. It's true what they say, you never know what's coming around the corner.

***

The dogs were very noisy and one morning I woke up feeling completely worn out. The pressure of taking over at the office and not sleeping well had got to me. I was hot and covered in sweat. I really didn't want to go to work, but Sean was in Bahrain and needed to get to Aramco for a meeting so I had agreed to give him a lift. I dressed and went to the kitchen, and when Kaitlin saw me she told me I looked very pale. I was shivering but it was a lovely day and really quite warm. I told her I needed to get to work and went off to collect John. He worked for one of my competitors but as a trainer rather than a salesman, and Aramco had already bought the other product so no problem with me. They had asked him to come for a day to go over some small discrepancies so I'd offered to help.

I didn't see how Sean would have got there without my lift, so I felt obligated. As I drove I was getting hotter and it was only my mind that kept me going. I should have asked him to drive but I wanted him to think I was just out of sorts and it was the beginning of a cold. Also, I needed to bring him back later that day.

During the drive Sean asked me if I was going to come back to Arabscan after my summer break or not. I told him I had agreed a two year deal and couldn't see me leaving with no job to go home to. He said he was setting something up with Angus and Shaikh Hmood, and would I consider joining them? I was so hot and beginning to feel sweaty and to be honest I wasn't in the right mood to think about changing my job, also I needed to concentrate on driving, so I told him I'd think about it and let him know later. Blimey, something else for me to deal with.

When I got to the office Hamid took one look at me and called Mr. Belali.

'Get him to the doctor right away,' Belali said.

'I'll be alright, ask Gopal to bring me some water and I'll go and rest in my office for a while.'

'You're going to the doctor for a check-up and to put my mind at ease,' Belali said. 'You don't look well at all, quite sick in fact.'

So Hamid called the driver Gufar, who drove me to the local quack. The waiting room was full of Indians and the doctor was also Indian. I was ushered to the front of the queue; well, it was more of a mob really.

'I'll wait my turn,' I told the guy taking names. I can't call him a receptionist as there was no reception desk to speak of.

'This is my manager so he must be before these workers,' said Gufar.

'OK, you're next,' said the name taker.

I was suitably embarrassed by this but I respected their case. I sweated another bucket while waiting my turn. When I eventually got to see the doctor, he was all panicky and ushered me into another room with a bed in.

'Take off your shirt and get on the bed,' he ordered me.

'OK, calm down doc, I'm feeling a bit hot that's all.'

'I'll be the judge of that,' he said.

He checked my pulse and looked in my mouth and measured my temperature and blood pressure.

'I need to check your stools,' he said.

'You have got to be joking, it's a cold,' I said.

'No joke, take this tube to the toilet. I need a sample.'

I came back with the sample and asked him, 'How long will this take? I need to get back to work.'

'It won't take long and I've already sent your driver back to tell them you're not coming back today.'

'You shouldn't have done that. I'm their manager and they will only worry more now.'

'So they should, if it's what I think it is.'

He was worrying me now, or should I say scaring or frightening even. I needed to get Sean back to Bahrain safely tonight, he hadn't got anywhere to stay otherwise. Also I'd got no way of getting a message to him.

Wow, I was really feeling shitty now. Next thing I knew the doctor had wheeled a drip into the room and connected me up to it.

'Do you have the results back so soon?' I asked.

'No, but I've a feeling that you need some saline and I'm taking no chances,' he replied. 'It will take your temperature down and make you feel better.'

Feel better, feel better. 'It's a cold,' I kept saying.

'We'll see, I'm not usually wrong,' he said.

'You haven't told me anything positive yet, you're getting me worried that's all.'

'Rest, I'll be back in a while. I've got people to tend to.'

So I was resting and worried about what could be wrong with me. I needed to get better quickly. After a short while, I'd probably dozed off a bit. He came and took my temperature which had come down to almost normal.

'You've got something we don't usually find in white people, you've got dysentery,' he said. 'It comes from poor hygiene in food preparation, do you remember where you've been eating recently? I can't believe it came from your own cooking.'

The only place I remembered was the curry I'd had out with Sean and Angus. I felt so much better and the doctor said I could go, but to be careful in future where and what I ate.

'Go home and drink lots of Pepsi Cola,' he said.

'Why?' I asked.

'Because it's full of sodium which is great for clearing out your stomach,' he replied.

I wasn't sure of that, but Coke wasn't a bad idea as I was quite parched. I called Hamid and he sent Gufar to collect me. When I got back to the office I had some tea and a large glass of water then rested until it was time to collect Sean and go home. I told him I would think about it seriously and let him know at the weekend. I had a couple of days at home building my strength back up. I stocked up on Pepsi and Coke, but Nick just added it to his Jack Daniels.

I met John, Angus and Shaikh Hmood at John's apartment on the Thursday night and we talked about the new setup. They were going to be based in Bahrain and run a data company servicing all the large companies with the help of Hmood's royal connections. I thought it sounded good, and spent nearly the whole weekend with them seeing what they had done so far. Hmood said he had a colleague who lived in Abu Dhabi and asked me if I would go with him next weekend to meet him and discuss the new venture. They certainly seemed to want me in on the deal, so I agreed.

***

It's a good job I kept those business cards because a couple of days later it paid off. Arabscan paid my wages monthly in cash and I couldn't get to the bank to pay it in, so I took it home. I planned to take it to the bank the next day. Just my luck, I was on my own when I crossed the bridge the following day and the Saudi customs guy wanted to check the whole car including my briefcase. He was so surprised to see so many riyals, he wanted to know how I got it and why I was carrying it into Saudi Arabia. I told him my story and he was very sceptical. He marched me into his hut and made me wait while he called his superior. After half an hour he was ignoring me and probably waiting for his boss, so I thought I'd get in first; at least he spoke English.

'I need to call my boss and explain why I'm going to be late,' I said. 'It might be too early to wake him so would you mind explaining for me?' I asked him.

'Give me his number,' he said.

Then I showed him my 'joker' card, or my 'get out of jail free' card if you like.

I had two to choose from, but I chose the 'Prince Turki' business card. I must admit I was hoping he didn't call him, and when he told me to go there and then I knew I had got away with it. I would keep Shaikh Hmood's for the opposite journey sometime.

First Class to Abu Dhabi

Shaikh Hmood called me saying he had a contact in Abu Dhabi who wanted to see my work. I was amazed that he would even think about me, let alone my work. Anyway, he wanted me to accompany him on a visit and show his mate what I had and we would take it from there.

We arranged to meet at the Holiday Inn hotel on Thursday morning and would fly to Abu Dhabi together. I was nervous to say the least. I drove there, parked, and waited in reception for him. He arrived in a brand new all-singing all-dancing Range Rover and he was covered in gold braid. Oh my God, I'm in the company of royalty again.

He drove to the airport and was really good company, chatting about the new venture all the way. The airport staff were all a fluster as if the king had arrived. He only had his own jet and it was first class travel, so for once in my life I wished the flight could have been longer. They even offered us champagne; Hmood had non-alcoholic, I had the real stuff.

I'd only been in a small plane a couple of times, one was when I'd worked in Barrow-In-Furness ten years ago and had flown from Biggin Hill airfield in Kent to Walney Island in Cumbria in a Grumman Tiger four seater and that had a propeller, just one.

It wasn't my first time in Abu Dhabi either, I'd been there a few years before with Ron. We'd had a call regarding some work for Adco (Abu Dhabi Oil Company). We'd been for a month in '92 and they wanted us back for a week.

Problem was they'd only pay for one person and Ron always wanted to go for a free week away. I don't think he trusted me to go on my own either. Only he couldn't do the job. So we did a deal and got a fixed price for the job. We organised a trip for two through a travel agent. It meant staying in the Chicago Beach Hotel just outside Dubai and driving to the office in Abu Dhabi each day. It was Ramadan so we made sure we had a big breakfast each morning at the hotel because we knew we couldn't eat at lunchtime. On the last day after we'd completed the work we went shopping then decided to eat in one of the top hotels. The food was great and the beer was served in teapots to disguise it.

After we finished we headed for the car only to find Ron had lost the keys. Great, it was nearly midnight, we were in Abu Dhabi, our flight was from Dubai at seven in the morning. We retraced our steps but no luck, we couldn't find them, so we went back to the hotel to ask for help. They were great and called the car hire company. After arguing for about ten minutes we threatened to smash one of the windows to get our bags and then get a cab back to our hotel. They went berserk and told us not to do that, and they would send a cab from Dubai to us with a spare set of keys. It was around midnight by now and he must have driven his Mercedes like a racing driver to get to us. He arrived around one am and it was our turn to drive like nutters, but we only had a Pontiac Firefly and not a Merc so we drove like a couple of rally drivers.

'Never again,' I said, but you never know.

Anyway, this was different; so me and my mate Shaikh Hmood landed in Abu Dhabi to a red carpet and bowing airport staff.

'We are so sorry, we weren't expecting you, sir, or we would have prepared better.'

I was following like a lamb.

'I'm with him,' I said.

He had ordered a limo and it was waiting for him at the door. We were off to another Holiday Inn, this one on the corniche.

There was none of the noise that was constant closer to the city; I had to strain to hear the sound of traffic a scant mile away. We went in to meet his contact and I wanted to get it over and done with as soon as possible. They wanted tea, Arabic tea, as it's traditional to greet royalty with a little something before discussing business.

I hoped I was not staring too much but I was thinking this bloke looked like a mafia guy, maybe his name was Don, dark hair, dark glasses, said he came from Sicily. He showed me some photos of him in his private jet. I mean, how much more mafia could you get?

I was thinking I should get a rate increase for all the stress. One minute I was with royalty and the next it was organised crime.

The fact was, he didn't need to be shown anything, he was having it anyway based on the say-so of Hmood, but I showed him anyway. I thought it went well, the relief showed all over my face, and my body relaxed when it was over. It was a jolly for us and we enjoyed our day out.

Lunch was a feast, slow roasted lamb. Hmood isn't a little guy nor was the Don; at least I wasn't paying. My second flight in a private jet was uneventful as both airports knew he was coming this time.

I thanked him for involving me in a 'royal experience', as I called it 'First Class'.

Home Again

During the summer Mr. Rebdi went on his yearly holiday to Al-Hasa, the largest oasis in the world, and some of the lads had vacation time. They hadn't been home for two years and it was important to get their flights arranged because all flights were booked up very quickly. The schools packed up for two months as it was too hot and the ex-pat children were all sent home. Half the country were leaving so I'd planned a day in the office to check stock of who was due time off and who would cover for them. It ran smoothly normally, but the summer months meant losing a few here and there for vacations and I had to plan them or we would be short in each department. I was stopped in my tracks when Hamad passed me a call from my wife and she told me that my father had died. Wow, what a shock; it was like a knockout blow. I had to get out of the office and find some space by myself. I had a small cry, told myself to get grip and came back to the office.

I had a meeting with Mr. Belali and after discussing this with him he agreed I could have a couple of weeks off. I told him I felt like staying there when I got home, but he thought it was mainly my grief talking. We called Mike in and explained and asked him to hold the fort while I was away. I left them and went to ask Hamad to get me on the first flight to Heathrow. All the guys knew something was up and wanted to know what had happened. I told them I was going home and Mike would be taking over so look after him.

I was so upset I thought I might not be coming back after this, I'd missed home a lot and this could be the final straw. It turned out Hamad couldn't get me a seat for four days as all flights were full, even connecting flights, so I had a few days to hand over to Mike and this kept my mind off the funeral.

Eventually Hamad got me a flight via Budapest, which was a pain but I had to take it. I had to wait four hours in a cold deserted transfer lounge for the connecting flight.

I arrived home to find my mum and my youngest brother Mark, who lived with them, really struggling to deal with the problems dad had left them. Mark also told me about some really spooky stuff that had affected him badly since dad had had his stroke three months before. Mark was in the Territorial Army and used to go on regular weekend camping trips. One evening while mum was at the hospital visiting dad, he was packing his stuff and he couldn't find his torch. Mum came home and told him that during the whole visit dad was frantic and kept pointing behind him towards his pillow and in broken speech kept saying, 'It's in there, it's in there.' Mark wondered about this, and when he went to bed that night he found his torch under his pillow.

During another visit dad was calling out for, 'Bobby,' 'Bobby,' 'Bobby.' When she arrived home Mark said, 'That damn parakeet was screeching all afternoon and he couldn't shut him up.'

'That's not all,' he said. 'That doorbell dad had fitted for his bad hearing hasn't worked from the day he went into hospital; it just stopped like it wasn't needed anymore.' Mark was getting the shakes as he said it.

'It's like he's been watching over us while he's been away and he knew he was dying,' he said.

My dad's watching over all of us like he always had, he was a wonderful man and I was going to miss him.

***

I was unsure about the future as we buried my dad and talked a lot with my family. My wife knew I had unfinished business, but my mum and four brothers were not sure why I wanted to go back. After all the stories I'd told them, they thought I was mad as a March hare; I probably am, there are quite a few in my family.

Mr. Rebdi called me the day after the funeral and said if I came back they would make me overall manager with total control of the office with an increased pay offer.

Guess what?

You don't have to guess. I'll tell you what happened, I accepted the offer.

This was the third time I chose to go, and this time I was going to make it work. Third time lucky, as the saying goes, but you make your own luck these days.

Part 3

Chapter 14

Come Together

I already had my visa so no problems with customs, so off we go again. A new day, a new mystery and as always, the sun was up, the sky was blue without a cloud in sight.

The first day back I got a big cheer from the lads and my office had been arranged for me. It was a big relief that they wanted me back and Mike welcomed me with open arms. He hadn't enjoyed the role when I was away, and thanked me for coming back to rescue him from Sala Baban, who had joined us full time. Seems like there's always someone needs rescuing. Mike had my old job as tech support manager and it suited him well. It was a promotion for him and it came with a pay increase and a new car. He had asked for a Toyota Camry, and surprisingly they had agreed. That's better than mine, I thought; well, good luck to him.

I wanted to work to get over my grief. I just needed to be busy and, most of all, I needed time. This time I was in charge of my accommodation allowance so I would choose where to live and make sure I budgeted better to have a better living style. I knew the rules now so living in Al-Khobar didn't faze me. I could pick a nice compound and have change for extras.

I said to Mike, 'When I left Dhahran last time I thought I'd never return, you know, after the things that happened at home.'

'I wondered about that too. Do you fancy some lunch? There's a small restaurant on my compound,' Mike asked me.

'OK thanks, that sounds nice, let's go.'

'How come Sala has joined us full time?' I asked him on the drive out.

'The Prince sacked him,' Mike said.

'Wow, that must have been a blow to him,' I said.

'Maybe but it doesn't show. He's been acting just the same, ordering us about,' he said. 'You can handle him, he respects you, but I'm fed up taking orders from him and I'm so glad you're back.'

The restaurant was in the centre of Arabian Village compound and it felt good to go and meet a couple of his friends. First impressions were OK and I liked the look of the place. The man who ran the restaurant was a Palestinian called Baha Abu Shamalla and he served a pretty good lunch. Baha's parents were lecturers at the university in Riyadh. They came to Saudi twenty-five years ago when Baha was five, and they'd stayed ever since. He said he felt like he had no country to call his own, so his parents had arranged a Jordanian passport for him or he couldn't have stayed in Saudi Arabia to work.

He was a handsome guy, over six feet tall with dark hair and an olive skin complexion. His always wore really smart clothes and everyone thought he should have been a movie star, and he never wore socks. He told me he'd been married twice and had two daughters with his first wife, Tara. He'd married her when she was fourteen and it was like having three kids to bring up. His second wife, Rina, was Jordanian and a bit older than him. They all lived together and he said Rina was in charge now. Mike and I liked him for his honesty, and I saw him at Tim's villa most weekends.

I chose Arabian Village because Mike and Vien lived there and it would be nice to have friends near for weekends. The rent was a lot less than the twenty five percent of my wages I was allowed, so I had a few bob in my pocket as well. Plus, the nurses from the local dentist lived there in the women's single section so I could get fifteen percent off any dental work I needed.

The compound was split in two halves, singles and families. There were apartments in the single section and some two-storey blocks. I had no choice but to choose a first floor one-bedroom apartment on the singles side of the compound. It had one large room with a curtain dividing the living area from the sleeping area. The shower, toilet and small kitchen were at the back overlooking a pool and terrace reserved for single men.

Mike had a three-bed villa on the family side. There were two large pools on his side but the only way to get to them was through the villas. I had to ask permission to visit Mike, but he always allowed me to come over and spend any evening or weekend at his place.

This time I was determined to do some cooking for myself and I had a lot of learning to do. Luckily most of the lads in the office could cook and they helped me no end. I needed a teacher.

Mike had an open house every Thursday evening and a few of the neighbours came by for an evening listening to rock music and playing darts. There were always lots of Americans at Tim's who were rubbish at darts, and ended up playing their guitars most of the night. We all sang along, a bit like backing singers. They let me be lead singer sometimes if it was a slow number. I'm not a bad crooner, especially after some Dutch courage.

Mike always had siddiqi, some white and some brown. He put Jack Daniels wood chips made from the barrels into the siddiqi and it stained it brown. I must admit I was quite tipsy, well OK, almost drunk but not quite, when I left each time. Baha didn't drink alcohol but he didn't care much if we did. I made a point of talking to him about living here and trying and get some cooking lessons. He advised me to try all sorts of easy dishes and it soon dawned on me Baha was so easy going he was good at most things. I had another idea and asked Tim's opinion.

'Do you think Baha would fancy a job at Arabscan? He's a good talker and I bet he's a good salesman. He would be perfect with the Arab community, he could charm the hind leg off a donkey I'm sure,' I asked him.

'That's all very well, but he's Palestinian and the Saudis don't trust them,' Mike replied.

'I'm going to ask Belali,' I said. 'Don't mention it to Baha yet though.'

'Of course, I think he will help you when you're out and about; he's been here forever and knows loads of companies,' Mike said.

Taking Over

About a month after I returned we heard that Princess Diana had been killed in a car crash in Paris. Her partner was Egyptian so the Arabic papers and television reported it daily. It seemed the whole world was in mourning and each of us had great sympathy with his and her families. The Saudi television companies even showed the funeral in Westminster Abbey.

It was amazing to see all my office staff, guys of all religions, feeling sad together about a Western princess. My team were making me feel really proud and their togetherness was so special. Even our boys in the site offices were talking about it when I visited them.

***

We had six guys from the Philippines working on site in an Aramco office in Abqaiq. I knew and liked all of them, and so much so I visited them frequently. I had a monthly meeting with the managers there so I always popped in to the office to see how they were. They shared an apartment there and only came to the main office once a month on payday. They were all great mates and worked as a team.

After I returned as manager Rolando hadn't returned from his vacation and had left a message that he wouldn't be coming back, so we needed a replacement in the Abqaiq office. While I'd been away Mr. Rebdi had chosen someone and told me to send him there as soon as possible. He'd instructed Azeer to organise his relocation, but as soon as I found out I pointed out the one big problem. He had chosen Fredrick, who was an Indian. I explained to Mr. Rebdi that the five boys already there were from the Philippines and they shared an apartment, which in my opinion was not really big enough for them as it was, let alone adding an Indian Muslim to the equation. Mr. Belali agreed with Mr. Rebdi and said these people work for us so they should be grateful for the work. If Fredrick was complaining he would talk to him. I told them Fredrick would never complain; it was not a matter of the work, but the problem lies with the accommodation. One thing I had learnt was you can't mix Christians and Muslims in an apartment. They are different cultures and have different needs. The only way to let Fredrick live there was to separate him from the others. I told Azeer to come with me to Abqaiq so we could discuss how we would partition the place so Fredrick would be OK.

Before we left I asked Hamid to make a list of guys that were friendly with the five left at Abqaiq. I'd never seen their apartment before and I was quite shocked to find it pretty small. They didn't want me to see it at first, until I pointed out we might get them some new things installed. The kitchen was in a terrible state, the hob had two broken rings, the threadbare carpet had seen better days and the shower was leaking.

Azeer knew all about it and told me they had caused it so they should clean it up. I thought these were young boys, some still in their teens, who were away from their parents and they needed help and I decided to help out but kept it to myself for now. We measured up and tried to make an extra room by dividing up a bedroom.

I think I knew what to do and it would not involve making a new room. When I got back to the office I asked Hamid for the list I'd asked him to prepare.

My next problem was telling Fredrick he wasn't going and choosing another guy. The thing was, Fredrick thought of it like a promotion because he was getting to go 'on site', as we call it. Another thing I'd learnt was the people working for me were extremely proud and they assumed they had upset me if I changed my mind about them.

I went home and concocted a reason for the switch in personnel. I'd made up my mind that Boyet, another Filipino, would be the new guy at Abqaiq and Fredrick would assume his role as squad leader in the main office. This would solve the accommodation issue and both would perceive it as promotion, whereas not a lot had changed otherwise.

When I explained this to Mr. Belali and Mr. Rebdi, they agreed and took the credit by saying they knew I'd come up with something. I was always trying to come up with something. I'd talked to all the lads in the office one to one in my office, and had got to know quite a lot about them.

Mac was indispensable, and the guys respected him immensely. I knew we needed to look after him or the office would fall apart. He'd worked at Arabscan for nine years and was very loyal to the owners. He had a wife and two children in the Philippines and he only went home for a month every other year so he had only seen his kids a few times through their entire life. I thought I knew a way of keeping him satisfied for a long time. I needed all the help I could get and this plan would help me and him. His vacation was due, so I asked Mr. Belali and Mr. Rebdi if we could maybe change his contract to a married man's status. They hadn't thought about it, typical I thought, but said they would discuss it. I explained the need for him to continue and the mess it would leave if he didn't return.

A few days later they called me in and told me their decision. They had both agreed to my suggestion, so would I tell him about it. I asked him to join me in my office and told him I had arranged for him to bring his family back with him after his vacation. I know it's a big thing, but he deserved to have them with him after the time he had put in. He was so overwhelmed he nearly broke into tears. It showed all over his face, he was grinning like a ginger cat. He thanked me and couldn't wait to call his wife. He went straight to Jaime's office to tell him. I knew I'd scored a few points with all the lads in the office that day.

I also kept thinking about the need to clean up the boys' apartment in Abqaiq, though, but I would come back to it later. It was a few days of stress for me and a lot of the new man management skills I'd learnt, so I was glad when it was over.

I remembered I'd planned to ask about Baha and called into Mr. Belali's office on my way to lunch. I knew he would be handing over to Mr Rebdi during the lunch break and would put it to him, to save me doing it twice. I explained that we missed Nick's salesmanship and it would help me to have an Arabic-speaking assistant to go to clients with. He would be great to have about the place too, a bit of a liaison. Mr. Belali liked the idea and promised to speak to Mr. Rebdi about it. He also asked me to call our representative in India about a replacement for the office. I'd been warned about this by John from Qatar.

I got hold of Mike.

'Come for a coffee at Shula,' I said.

'Great idea let's go,' he said.

When we got there, we were walking through the shopping area towards café at the centre when I stopped short and turned to Mike and said, 'There's someone standing by the counter at the café I don't really want to meet.'

'OK, do you want to go somewhere else?'

'No, let's see if he wants to talk.'

As we approached I called out, 'Hi Mosem.'

He looked shocked when he saw us and had what seemed like fear in his eyes. He recovered quickly and by the time we reached him he had composed himself.

'Mr. Dennis, I thought I'd never see you again,' he said.

'Well I told you never say never again, didn't I?'

'When did you come back?' he asked.

'A little over a year ago, where have you been?' I asked.

'I've been in Cairo.'

'How come? I thought you were working for Saud.'

'I left him last year, he was very upset with me when you left.'

'Well you were very much one of the reasons I chose to go like I did.'

'I was only doing my job.'

'You should have trusted me more.'

'It is in our nature not to trust many people, it is the Egyptian way.'

'Anyway, how is Azira?' I asked him.

'She has sent me away, so I have lost everything, I can only come back because I have a dual passport, so I can look for work.'

'I am sorry for Kaisa to be away from her father, but you reap what you sow in my book,' I said.

He drank his coffee and left.

'So that was the Mosem you told me so much about,' said Mike. 'He looks so tired and sad.'

'Well, he is a sly person and to keep it up tires you out, I bet he will run to Saud and tell him he saw me, and hope he gives him his job back,' I said, 'it's just what he would do.'

'Saud knows you're here, doesn't he?' said Mike.

'Of course he does, he signed a paper to allow me to come back, I carry it everywhere, but Mosem doesn't know that.'

'So do you think he will try to stir up trouble?'

'I wouldn't put it past him.'

'Anyway, let's drink to our health, not his,' said Mike.

'I've got to call India and organise a replacement for Boyet.'

'Good luck with that then,' Mike said.

'Yes I know what you mean, my friend John from Qatar told me to be careful, he interviewed a man over the phone once and it was one of the funniest things I'd heard of, apparently the guy being interviewed had sounded very confident over the phone and John had asked him to email his resume. When it arrived he'd stated he had passed exams in penmanship and lettering, and had a certificate for an under 15 colouring competition.'

Mike nearly choked on his soggy biscuit.

A bid in Jubail

We were on the preferred list at Hadeed, the Saudi steel company based in Al Jubail.

They didn't just give work out, you still had to bid for it, but only amongst the preferred consultants. All bids were closed and had to be submitted in sealed envelopes. I went to a bid meeting and chatted with the other bidders while the project leader opened each bid and compared them. We all drank Turkish coffee and waited while the Hadeed team discussed the bids. We all knew that they would have already checked each company out to see if they were capable of completing the work.

By the time they returned we were all buzzed up with caffeine. When they returned, they asked their preferred top three bidders to remain and the others to leave. I was one of the top three this time. They asked each one of us how we could prove to them we were the best candidate for this work. This was like an interview, and it was the most nerve racking situation I'd been in at Arabscan. After our explanations they retired to discuss. They returned again and asked one other to leave. The project leader then told the remaining two of us, in a roundabout way, if we adjusted our price we could win the bid. It was up to us to re-submit our bids and he would choose. I didn't know how much the other bid was for so I had to guess.

We won the bid to scan their entire hand drawn documents into digital format. Now my problems started. They didn't want us to remove any documents from their premises, so this meant sending four of my guys to the Hadeed office.

I went back to my office and told Mr. Rebdi, who told me he knew we would win.

'Come off it, how did you know?' I asked him.

'Because it was our turn,' he said.

'What do you mean our turn, do you mean all that work I did preparing the bid was a waste of time?' I asked.

'No, we always have to go through the motions and put in a bid, but they always share it round amongst the companies so everyone keeps busy, they owed us some work,' he said. 'Some companies know they are not going to win and some don't want to win.'

'I checked your bid and so did Mr. Belali and we knew it was a bit high but that was OK, we wanted some negotiating room. We always have to reduce the cost so we're happy.'

'By the way, will you bring that salesman in please we'd like to talk to him?' he said. 'I know you know him so it's not like an interview.'

'Thanks, he'll be happy to see you too,' I lied.

I'd better make sure he wants the job first, I thought.

It's OK winning the work and you know you'll get paid because it would cause outrage if they defaulted, but they wouldn't pay for ninety days. We had to make quite a lot of upfront payments.

It was too far to travel each day, so we had to find accommodation for four men. This was another one of my mistakes. Out of my list of six candidates I didn't account for status. This is another big difference between my usual working environments. Religion is a big factor, but age comes into it as well.

I had learnt something though, my new team of Hadeed guys were all Indian. This kind of helped me but I hadn't planned on the 'age thing'.

Abel was the smartest but the laziest, Thomas was the quickest but made mistakes, Ajay was the youngest but steady and reliable and Jojo was the oldest but the slowest.

Anyway Azeer had the task of finding some place for them to live during the project. There were plenty of camp sites in Jubail for workers, but because Mr. Belali was all about making profit he wanted the cheapest place. He had no people skills in my opinion because he didn't much care about them. They were just workers and should be grateful for the job.

I disagreed with him, because I always ascertain people work better if their home life is good. Anyway, he found them somewhere to live, I had a look and it was a dump.

I was getting familiar with the way of life in Saudi nowadays, and one day on my way back to the office from Jubail I saw a man waiting by the roadside. I stopped and asked him if he needed help, he said he was OK, so I asked him if I could drop him anywhere. He looked surprised but accepted and on the way we chatted about what we had been doing that day. I asked him where he was going and he wanted to be dropped off at a small village called Umm Al Sahik, near Safwa, not far from the main road and about half my way home. I'd never been there before so I asked him to show me the turn-off. When we got there I insisted on taking him home. He sounded a little more surprised but said OK. He directed me to his house and when we got there he invited me in. His wife was surprised – a lot of surprises so far – to see him so early. She wanted me to stay for tea and evening dinner but I declined and said I needed to get home myself. He was so grateful he gave me a packet of spices and a big box of dates, from his garden he said.

I told the guys in the office and they went mental.

'Are you mad? You should never do that, you could be kidnapped, assaulted or robbed,' they all chimed up together.

I was OK though, he was nice and thankful and I'm glad I could help him out. As I said, I was feeling much safer out there and I knew there were some nice honest guys on the streets just content on working for their families.

***

I went round to the café on the compound and found Baha. I offered him a job at Arabscan assisting me with sales. It would mean visiting clients and preparing quotations. He was taken aback by my offer and asked for some time to discuss it with Rina.

'You can get someone to manage this place, there are plenty of guys looking for an opportunity like this,' I told him.

'It doesn't work like that, Mr. Dennis,' he said. 'I have to talk to the owners first and they will need to replace me. Your offer is amazing and I promise to give you an answer in a couple of days. Rina will be very happy I think.'

Please don't let me down, I was thinking. I've been telling my bosses you're the missing link. I gave him all the time he wanted as long as he told me by the weekend.

***

Nick and Gianni invited us to the Middle East trade show in Dubai again as the Saudi Arabian representatives for both our dealerships. I would be on one stand with Gianni and Mike would be on the other with Nick.

It was school half term the week before the show, so I asked for a week's break to be with my family. My wife booked a self-catering package holiday to Crete. I arranged to meet them there as it would be crazy for me to fly home and us all to go together. They would go from Gatwick airport in London. It sounds easy to say 'I'll meet you there', but not for me. The usual round-about way of getting somewhere. I had to catch an evening flight on Saudia Airlines to Riyadh, wait half the night then change to Olympus airlines to Athens, wait again then on a small plane to Heraklion. When I got to Heraklion I asked at information for directions to Amoudara. I was told to catch the bus outside and it would take around twenty minutes. I asked the driver to let me know when we had arrived. He did, so I got off and walked along the main street of the village looking for anything open so I could ask for direction to my accommodation, but it was siesta time and nothing was open. It was very hot in the middle of the day and I was exhausted. I found a small café, had a drink and asked where to find Virginia apartments. Nobody had heard of them but the taxi office next door maybe had. I finished my coffee and went and asked. Nobody had heard of the place. Have you tried the other Amoudara, one guy said. You are joking, there's two? He called another cab firm and they said it was indeed on the other side of the island. They offered to take me for seventy euros. That is extortion, I thought. So, no choice again, let's go. It took about an hour to get there so that was why it was so costly. I got there and thanked him. I needed a rest so I went to check in. The receptionist wasn't expecting me until the following morning so my room wasn't ready. Great. I was so tired, but they offered me a Greek salad on the house and said my room would be ready in about an hour. It was such a beautiful day and I was on holiday, so I sat on the terrace looking out to sea with the best salad in my life and a gin and tonic without a care in the world for a few hours, at peace. When my room was ready I crashed out for a few hours. At around six o'clock I remembered I was supposed to get some food and drink for the children when they arrived, so I walked to the small town and bought some orange juice and local bread and cheese. They wouldn't be arriving until the early hours of the morning, so I watched the sun go down and had an early (ish) night, excited to see them again. When their coach arrived I was awoken by the tour guide and when she opened the door with her key. She screamed the place down when she saw me in my pyjamas and standing by the door. My wife assured her it was me, and she left in a state of shock I expect. I was awake and wanted to see them but they were sleep walking and just wanted to get to bed.

It was wonderful to see them away from home and enjoying the island. It was pretty cold in England, so the sun was doing them some good too. We had a fabulous holiday and visited all the famous sites. My youngest son Philip was doing a project on Greek mythology so he was buzzing all week.

I had to leave a day before them because of all the connections and time it took to get to Dubai. Nothing simple in my life lately. That was a joke too, firstly a taxi to the airport and the driver wasn't in a rush even though I was. The flight from Heraklion to Athens was so late it was eventually cancelled, which left me arguing at the check in desks because I was going to miss my connection. They made me wait for what seemed like hours, but was probably only one. Eventually they found me a seat on a Swissair flight and I had to run for it. Luckily, I only had a carry-on bag. I made it, just. At least I had a hotel in Dubai and they were expecting me. I needed a morning to get over the time difference, but I got to the show and Mike was there with Nick and Gianni. Back to work for some rest and normality. A good week, loads of business and some people to get back to when we got back to the office.

Chapter 15

West and North

Jeddah Again

I got a call from the head of development in Sabic. We'd met at the Riyadh engineering show and I'd bumped into him again in Dubai. He asked me to visit him at the Sabic main development offices in Jeddah. Well, it was an extremely important call and I knew it could set us up for a long future. I've said before Sabic are almost the biggest company in the Middle East, and this guy was their chief honcho in development.

Both Mr. Belali and Mr. Rebdi agreed with me and told me to go and take anyone from the office team with me. I chose Jaime, who was the best programmer we had, and let Azeer organise our trip. It would be Jaime's first trip outside the eastern province so we needed a special dispensation letter and a stamp in his iqama. I'd been before so mine would still be valid.

To say he was excited was an understatement. He nearly wet himself when I told him we were going. He said he'd never stayed at a 'posh' hotel before.

Baha had agreed to join us and had settled in well, so I left him in charge while we were away. I was allowed to claim our expenses back from the company so I made sure we spent wisely and made a profit on the deal. Jaime was a typical Filipino who wanted rice with every meal, but I talked him into a Western style dinner and breakfast for once. I told him to write up an expense form for it all even though he didn't pay anything towards it. I gave the money we made to the boys in Abqaiq to buy a new carpet.

***

I was looking forward to getting home at the weekend because the FIFA confederations cup was being held in Saudi and it was being shown live on TV. It was impossible to get a ticket to a match but Arabian Village had Star Sports dishes, so I could watch as many games as I liked. This would have included a bit of skiving off in England, but thankfully the matches were played in the evening due to the heat.

It had previously been known as the King Fahd Cup and this was the first time it had been endorsed by FIFA so some other confederations were included. The Saudis weren't the best at football and the commentators all spoke Arabic, but they had invited Brazil who were the current world champions so it was going to be great to watch. The Saudis' group included Mexico and Australia as well as Brazil. Every match was being played at the King Fahd II stadium in Riyadh, called the 'Pearl' in Arabic. The king even had a royal balcony added for him to sit and watch the game, away from the main supporters.

I headed to Mike's place because he had the largest lounge, the largest TV and siddiqi. There was quite an audience including Mike, Baha and a couple of Mike's neighbours, a Scotsman named Stuart and an American called Jerri and even Vien's Thai friend Jonu. Stuart lived next door and had brought some home brew which was like an English ale, except much stronger. Nobody could tell how strong it was, though. Jerri always visited at the weekends and wasn't that interested in the football, or soccer as he called it. Not enough scoring, you couldn't pick the ball up and it was the wrong shape he reckoned. Jonu ran an illegal lottery amongst the Thai community and wanted to take bets on the result, so we all bet a few riyals each.

'This is the best Brazil side I've ever watched,' I said.

'Yes, they have such a great flow about them,' said Baha.

'Hey Jerri, at least they are the champions of the whole world, and not the world champions of the USA like your lot.' I was in a funny mood after some of Mike's sid and coke.

'They'll have to watch out for Ronaldo,' Mike said.

'The team is full of guys to watch out for,' I told them. 'What about Romario or Rivaldo?'

'I bet the Saudis don't score against that Brazilian defence,' Jonu said.

Jonu wanted to take more bets on the game that night, but we were all too merry and Baha wouldn't gamble because he said it was against his religion. No sense of humour, either, that's his problem.

The Saudis looked a bit overawed by the Brazilians and lost three nil in the first match in front of 50,000 home supporters. They managed only one win, one nil, against Australia after losing their other group match five nil to Mexico, and were knocked out of the competition without getting out of the group. Maybe Jerri was right where Saudi Arabia were concerned.

Ramadan January '98

Ramadan arrived and some of our guys have been given permission to go on a pilgrimage to Mecca. It was my first man hour problem, as we were short staffed for a month. I had to ask the guys in each office to double up and do longer shifts to cover for the guys that are away. There was a bit of resentment around the place so I called a general meeting. The whole country had slowed to walking pace and I had to explain that we would reimburse guys who were covering. This put the back up of the guys doing prayer time, who could not put in the same hours. It was a problem that couldn't be solved, as it was bringing religion into the day to day. It showed where the shortcomings were in having a multi-cultural office, but it couldn't be helped.

I wasn't the first manager to have this problem and I won't be the last. I was sympathetic to both sides but unless everyone is doing the same amount of work we were always going to have disputes. I asked Mr. Belali for advice as he was the best man to talk to about it. We end up changing the rota and dividing the time up amongst the remaining staff; it was only temporary anyway. I ended up helping out with the driving as we only had one driver available to get the Aramco shifts to and from the site office.

After Ramadan finished, we had a few days off for the Eid celebrations, which I spent with Mike, Vien and Philip. I got to know Baha more and found him to be a really knowledgeable man.

Mike came to work on the Saturday after Ramadan finished and told us that Jonu had been arrested during the festivities. He'd been involved in a road accident, the police searched his car and found a lot of money on him; there was no way he could explain it was the Thai lottery money from the weekend. He worked as an office cleaner so there was no way he could have saved so much money. As it is illegal to gamble in Saudi, the money was confiscated and he was sent to prison.

I knew all about the Thai gambling problems and I reckon he could have been involved in match fixing in London. There had been an evening game in November involving West Ham United and my team Crystal Palace where the lights had gone out with the score at 2-2. The match had been abandoned and millions of pounds had been paid out because it was ended as a draw. It had happened again at Crystal Palace's ground in December, when Wimbledon were playing Arsenal with the same outcome. The syndicate who arranged for the lights to go out were only caught when a security guard had informed the police of a third attempt at a Charlton Athletics match against Liverpool.

Chapter 16

Out and About

A Drive to Riyadh

How on earth do you find a place you need without a map written in English? Riyadh is 400km in area, and has a population of over 6 million and twenty governorates. Still, I had to take four of my team there for a secondment to the department of the interior. We had won a project to convert some documents to digital. I needed a map but I couldn't read the place names in Arabic, so I decided to take Julian, who could read a bit of Arabic and was the most sensible Filipino in the office behind Mac. It would be a shame to lose him from the main office, but I needed a strong person to run the new site office. Also he had been before and would be my guide when we got to Riyadh. He was a great guy to talk to and his opinions were greatly appreciated. He taught me a lot about the team and the main culture from the Philippines. I chose two Filipinos and two Indians, and all four got on well together which would be a great help to me. When we got there and found the main office, we were shown the office we had been allocated. It would do for my guys, as they were not thought of by the ministry very well. They were used to Saudis working in their offices. I assured them this was our best team and would give them no trouble. We were allowed to go and find our accommodation. We found the block which was full of apartments. Theirs had two big bedrooms with twin beds, so two in each and good for sharing. I said I thought it was really nice and wished I had it in Al-Khobar. All the lads said I should stay the night with them, but I was going to leave for my hotel. They persuaded me to stay and I cancelled the hotel booking and we went out for dinner. Julian suggested we go to the part of town where the majority of the Filipinos congregated. The Indian guys went to their own side and probably had curry. I went with Julian and he took me to a place a bit like Chinatown in London. All the restaurants were Filipino and he chose a good one. It was like a café but teeming with young people. I felt a bit like the odd one out but Julian told me not to worry. The food smelt good but looked weird. He said I should try a delicacy called fish cheeks. Oh my God, are you joking? I didn't fancy that at all. Still, in for a penny; I let him order for me and when it came I was pleasantly surprised, it was deep fried and looked like the fish and chips from I get in England. Obviously you can't see the fish under the batter, but it tasted fine. What a relief! I will never question these guys again, they certainly know about food. We went back to the apartment and they insisted I have the biggest room to myself.

'Don't be silly, there are two beds in there and you can't all go in the other room,' I argued.

'We'll be fine, you must have the room to yourself,' they all said.

'Really, we'll make it work, we usually do,' was their answer.

So I got the big room with a really comfortable bed. They were going to think it was heaven when they got in there, I thought.

That was the night I started having bad dreams about being lost in the desert looking for my way home. It kept occurring;

I'd be with somebody and I'd stop to look at something and when I looked up I was alone. I kept running around trying to find the person I'd lost but it was me who was lost, until I woke up.

I was feeling guilty leaving those young lads in the big city to fend for themselves. They put me to shame, the way they had no fear being so far from home and family. The following day it was the Indian guys' turn and they took me to lunch. They first picked a McDonald's burger bar but I refused and asked to go for a traditional curry. They thought that was what I would like, but not me. We ended up in an Indian type café and they ordered my meal of mutton curry and rice. It was delicious and I was thankful it wasn't too hot for my taste.

I took them to the office and had a short meeting to make sure they knew what was needed then I went out to explore Riyadh. Some of the buildings were very futuristic; the government building was like a spaceship, the ground floor was narrower than the top floor like it was upside down.

I drove home by myself in the afternoon and prayed I'd make it without the dream coming true.

I'd slept badly and needed some exercise so I took to the pool the next day and tried to swim some lengths when a man appeared alongside me. He'd seen I was tiring and he coaxed me to continue to the side of the pool. I'm not a very strong swimmer and he had helped me get there. When we got to the side he asked me if I'd been here long and told me he was new to the place. He introduced himself as Darren and said he was from Oldham in Lancashire. I had an aunt that lived there once and four cousins that were born there so I knew where it was, although I hadn't been there in a long time. He worked as a quality assurance specialist, although I'd not seen much quality around here since I'd arrived, so he had a job for life if he could stand it. It was good to know I was not the only single British guy living on the compound. He asked if I fancied a drink that evening, and I thought I could murder a beer so I accepted. I went round and met a few of his mates. It was similar to

Neil and Simon's place but not as well done, just someone's front room, but they had sid and homemade beer. So it made a change to have some new people to talk to. A couple were into running and they invited me to a hash run one Friday soon. I'd not heard of hash running but it sounded interesting and fun. I agreed to go with them the following weekend.

Back to Bahrain

While I was in England I arranged a meeting with Ron and as he couldn't come to Saudi without a sponsor, I said I'd come to Bahrain for a weekend. On the Wednesday I was going, I came to work as usual and had planned a day in the office so as not to get caught up anywhere. Mike was still waiting for his new car; it was so new it hadn't even arrived in the Kingdom yet. So he asked to borrow mine. As I wasn't going out I thought it would be OK. He was only going downtown to get something for his wife's birthday. Anyway, he went and I got on with some paperwork, mostly appraisals, which was another new thing for me to deal with. About an hour later, I got a message from Azeer that Mike was at the police station. Apparently, someone had driven into the back of my car on the exit ramp of Shula carpark. What the! I called the police station and got through to my mate the chief, who told me he would call me back. He did and said Mike was OK but he was being accused of stalling the car, and the other guy thought it was Mike's fault, but he'd sort it out for me. Mike came back soon after and thanked me for getting him out.

'I thought I was going to have to stay in for the night,' he said, which would have meant the weekend because nothing gets done at the police station over the weekend. Anyway, now I needed a car for my weekend. It was too late to cancel, Ron would be in the air now on his way. So Hamid and Azeer between them persuaded Mr. Rebdi to agree I could borrow the Land Rover Discovery we had as a spare vehicle; still no Rav4. It meant getting special insurance documents from the chamber of commerce with my details, as I wanted to take it to Bahrain. What a palaver, now the rush was on. Azeer took me with a signed letter from Mr. Rebdi to get it approved. We had to go to Dammam; I was glad it wasn't a Friday, they had beheadings in the main square on Fridays. It was pandemonium in the main hall at the chamber of commerce but Azeer knew just about everyone there so he signalled someone and they jumped him to the front. When he explained the emergency they issued a license immediately. On the way back we stopped at my place for my weekend bag.

I got going but the car was a brute with a dodgy gearbox. It was meant to be four-wheel drive but it wouldn't change from two to four so I nursed it over the causeway. Ron didn't recognise me when I met him at the airport that night; he was looking for a skinny white guy driving a white Toyota, and he got a tanned tubby bloke in a big people carrier. I had booked us into the Mansouri Mansions aparthotel in separate rooms. At least it had a bar and some great Mediterranean food on the menu.

He explained that the London office was struggling and having to close, so he'd brought papers for me to sign. It was a sad day, that our dream of a company that would outlive us and we could pass to our children was dying. Still, it was better than us all getting dragged down with it. They had arranged to sell it to the sales team so we would be out of it. Ron wanted to carry on by himself, but his brother Laurence and Martin had to look for new jobs. They assumed I was going to be OK working here. We actually got drunk that night, the first time for me in quite a while. The next day I took him on a tour of the island and showed him the tree of life and we ended up at the Amir's beach.

The end of the World

I got stuck in again and arranged a few visits when I got back. One was to a Sabic office in Yanbu by Medina, on the west coast of Saudi. It is said that Yanbu is not the end of the world, but 'you can see the end of the world from there'.

King Fahd had commuted the sentences of the two British nurses accused of murder and this reminded me I needed to return to the Fahd military hospital; this time I took Baha with me. They had installed a newfangled fingerprint machine that had a small scanner inside to check our finger prints with a camera that took our picture. All new to us, very sophisticated and I supposed expensive. A security guy ushered us into a room at the back of the hospital.

'We need to take your finger prints before we can allow you into the data vault,' he said.

Wow, this was a seriously big deal for Baha, he'd never had his finger prints taken before, neither had I for that matter; but I explained we needed the work so there was not much choice. Our finger prints were recorded and we were issued with security passes. Baha was bothered about the 'Americans' having his fingerprints and his photo.

'You can come and go anytime from now on as your prints are stored,' the security guard said.

We managed to persuade them we could do exactly what they wanted and went back to prepare a quotation. All the guys in the office said Baha was getting a bit paranoid about his identity being stored but to my mind it didn't really matter.

A few days later he brought his wife Rina to the office to meet us and she told me she worked at the hospital as a nurse. She'd worked there for so long, she knew everyone. One of her best friends was Amit, a tailor who made the uniforms for the staff. That fascinated me, I'd never thought about their clothing before. She said he even embroidered their names on their tunics.

'So being a tailor, can he make a suit?' I asked.

'I will ask him but I would think it's possible,' she said.

'Thanks that would be great.'

'Just bring in one of your suits and I will take it to him to measure,' she said. 'He can make it the same size, I think you would look great in dark blue with your blond hair.'

The next day I brought my best suit in and Baha took it home for her.

A couple of days later he brought both suits back with a little present: it was a black baseball cap with the Crystal Palace F.C. badge embroidered on the front and my name on the side. I was overwhelmed with the quality and speed with which he had done it.

'How did you know about the badge?' I asked him.

'It was on the polo shirt you sometimes wear on weekends, I got Mike to "borrow" it so we could copy the crest.'

'I wondered where it was, I thought I'd left it at the laundry. It is special and I'll wear it to all the matches to remind me of you lot, how much does he want for it?' I asked.

'Four hundred and seventy five riyals, that is about sixty eight of your pounds, for the suit. Nothing for the cap, it is a present,' said Baha.

'You've got to be joking, is that all?' I couldn't believe it. It was so good.

'He will be offended if you offer more, he wants to do it for Rina and you,' he said.

'Done deal,' I said.

I still couldn't believe it.

***

He said there was a dance at the weekend and invited me, I accepted and went along. Mike and Vien were going and most of their friends, mostly Thai and Filipinos that I'd met at Mike's place. It was meant to be a secret because there would be alcohol there and Western music. It was in fact like a disco but with live Filipino singers, who were really good. I stood with Baha by the makeshift bar and watched the people dancing.

'Look at those girls dancing together in the middle, they are really beautiful,' I said.

'Dennis, they are the cooks from the Bangkok restaurant, they are both men,' said Baha.

'You can't be serious.' I was astounded.
'Be careful who you dance with, you'll be surprised,' he said.
'I won't be dancing, Baha, don't worry.'

My eyes were popping out so I just drank myself silly instead.

I had a sore head in the morning on the Monday. My weekly project meeting on Wednesday at Hadeed was eventful as I had to collect my team's timesheets. To save me some time I had asked Ajay to collect them and be ready when I came to get them. In my eyes this was working and all was OK for the first couple of visits, but on the third Monday I received a letter from Ajay via our receptionist Hamid. It appeared the other three were not talking to him and he blamed me.

His letter said they weren't talking to him and refused to pass their timesheets to him. They had effectively 'sent him to Coventry' as we say in the UK. I went for my usual visit and after my project meeting I went to our site office to collect the timesheets. I had made up my mind not to make a big thing of it so as not to cause Ajay more problems. The others didn't know he'd written to me.

'Is everything OK here?' I asked.
'Everything all OK, Mr. Dennis,' said Jojo.
'Well, it doesn't seem the way to me,' I said.

I decided to leave if for a few days and go back to head office and ask advice. I asked for the timesheets and Ajay told me he didn't have them. When I asked why, he said they wouldn't give them to him. I asked them all why, and JoJo said they wouldn't work for him and I shouldn't have put him in charge.

'Nobody's in charge,' I said, 'it's just easier for me to collect them from one person than going to everyone individually.'

They sheepishly gave me them individually and I told them I wasn't happy and I'd be back on Monday for a special visit to sort out the problems. I drove back thinking about how I was going to solve this new problem. When I got back to my office, I asked Hamid if he knew about the problems at Hadeed.

Of course, Hamid knew all about it and explained. This is where I learnt some more cultural things and I found out I'd got my selections totally wrong. Firstly, even though they were all Indian, I had chosen three Muslims and one Christian. I didn't realise and frankly I'd not even thought about it. My second miscalculation was I had not considered he was the youngest. Hamid wasn't only the office receptionist/secretary, he was also their token father. He was their agony aunt and they told him everything.

'You need to change one of them, Mr. Dennis,' he said.

'But I want the best team because they are away and I need to trust they will work without supervision,' I said.

'Well, I think we bring back Abel and replace him with Subir,' he suggested.

'Why Subir? Won't that make it worse?' I asked.

'No, Subir is a Christian and so is Ajay, then you will have two and two so Ajay will have a friend and he will feel better,' he explained.

'But when we bring Abel back he will feel disgraced, won't he?' I asked.

'Not if you make him squad leader of the new Sabic project that we are starting next month,' he replied.

'That's crafty and it will work,' I said.

'So I will organise it with Azeer and the boys, you don't have to worry,' he said.

'No, it has to come from me so when I go next week I'll tell them what is happening,' I said. 'Can I ask you to keep it between us till I let everyone know what we're doing?'

'Of course, and may I suggest you ask JoJo to collect the timesheets, he is the oldest and they have to respect him,' he said.

'Thanks Hamid, I've learnt another cultural thing that's not considered in my country,' I said.

I went home after the long day out driving and thought there were always going to be problems.

Even though Abel was lazy, he had a knack of managing, they seemed to look up to him, so it ended up being a win-win situation for the office and everyone involved.

Except me; I was getting fed up sorting out petty squabbling between the guys over religion, class, age and nationality.

A Sand Run

Darren knocked on my door and invited me to 'The Hash', as he called it. I remembered talking about it a few weekends before but I wasn't sure what it was, but he said it was fun and boy, I needed some. He arrived after lunch on Friday and offered to drive us to the meeting. It was out towards Half Moon Bay and it was a desert run. I used to play a bit of football and could run about the pitch OK, but I hated training including all the running it entailed. I don't mind short bursts but I'm crap at cross country. I used to do it at school but never on sand. When we arrived there were about twenty four-by-fours with all sorts of people falling out of them. I counted over fifty and they were all togged up in running gear, unlike me; I was dressed in t-shirt, smart shorts and old trainers. This was all new to an uneducated guy like me. Darren explained there was a guy called a runner who laid a trail and everyone else including me were the hounds and we had to follow his trail. Sounded easy to me, just look for the bits of paper he left behind. It didn't matter to me, though, because I wouldn't be first so I only had to follow along with the stragglers. Also, there were a few women who were out for a 'Sunday stroll' so I joined them and let the serious ones to find the 'Hare'. We came in almost last, but I enjoyed the company and had chatted all the way.

We were all invited back to the organisers villa after for drinks and a bar-b-que, so it would be rude not to go. Then they told me about the 'down-down'. It is a means of punishing, rewarding, or merely recognising an individual for any action or behaviour according to the customs or whims of the group. Because it was my first time and the fact that I didn't try very hard, I was asked to drink my pint of home brew in one go or risk pouring the remaining contents over my head. I managed about half and got a beer shampoo, but Darren was right, it was all good fun in the end.

It's Time to go

I thought about my children; my daughter was seventeen and good enough for university but couldn't decide whether to go there or to college, my eldest son was fourteen and starting GCSEs and then A levels, and my youngest son was eleven and getting ready for senior school.

I thought I'd had enough and decided I would leave for good at the end of my contract. I had a chat with Mike and Baha at Mike's one weekend and told them I wouldn't be back after the summer. They both said they understood as I had family back home and they didn't, but they still tried to persuade me to change my mind. The office was running well, and I thought I could leave it to Mike and Baha and not worry. We had become good friends as well as colleagues. I called my wife, telling her I was giving in my notice.

The next morning at work I told Mr. Belali and offered to work three months' notice and leave in the summer. Mr. Belali respected my decision and knew why I had made it. He said he was sad but knew his office would be OK with the guys left behind. He asked me to do him a favour and meet someone at the airport and take him to dinner after dropping him at his hotel. Of course, I agreed and asked him about it. He had made a few calls to England and wanted to partner with a company. Their managing director was coming to talk about the deal. I went and met the person and it was only the Managing Director of Electrowatt, a really big electrical company from England. They specialized in HVAC (Heating Ventilation Air Conditioning), electrical-mechanical, plumbing, extra low voltage systems and fire alarms and fire-fighting. This was a something I didn't expect. Gregory Wander was a very well-to-do person, beautiful suit and tie, smart shoes and an air of importance about him. I felt a bit overwhelmed by him actually, in fact he was a bit stuffy. There I was dressed in casual clothes to suit the warm evening, cream linen trousers, no jacket or tie. I dropped him at the Meridian and waited until he'd checked in then we went into town to one of the best Thai restaurants I could find. He talked about partnering with Arabscan and wanted to know my opinion. I didn't know anything about it and explained I was only the manager and had no dealings with the main partners about this sort of thing. The talk changed to our lives, which were so different, although we were both managing people. He relaxed and loosened his tie, eventually taking it off with his jacket.

'It's really warm here, I didn't realise how hot the evenings would be,' he said.

'This restaurant has air conditioning, you should know all about that and it's the evening, you wait until tomorrow,' I said. 'I'm sure that is why Mr. Rebdi and Mr. Belali want to meet you.'

'In this heat you couldn't be without it for long,' he said.

'If they could offer aircon they could make a fortune,' I said, 'we have a design office so we could offer solutions for fire safety as well.'

I told him this deal would probably be my last big one as I was leaving. He asked me what I would go home to, and I said I hadn't planned anything yet. Anyway, to me I had come so far from that council estate in Croydon to taking managing directors out for dinner.

I collected him the next day and took him to meet Mr. Belali. He stayed all day discussing a deal and I took him back to the airport that night. In the terminal we shook hands and he surprised me by offering me a job at his company. I took his business card and said I would call him when I got home, and I did.

***

I wanted to run the time down without any fuss but it wasn't going to be easy. I was busy looking at the end of year appraisals when Hamad called me to say I had a visitor in reception. I went to the lobby to find a man sitting in our reception area looking calm and collected. I asked him what I could do for him and he introduced himself as Faizan Al Basi, and that he worked for a firm of debt collection agents. Apparently, I owed some money to one of their clients and he had come to collect it from me. I was astounded and said I didn't know anything about this and asked him where this had come from. He said I owed Saud Al Harbi seventy thousand riyals, and when could I pay it back. It was like a slap in the face to me; I must have looked ashen. He knew I knew what he was referring to and waited for my reply. Obviously, I was a bit thrown by his accusation and had to think how I was going to deal with him. My partnership had been sold and there was no way to get the others to pay this back. I told him it had been a business transaction between Saud and my old company Online Design Limited, so he couldn't come to me individually. I explained the company was sold, but I was there so I suppose he had to try. I showed him the letter from Saud, informing anyone who was concerned that he had no problem with me. I asked him to go back to Saud and tell him I wouldn't be paying. I tried to keep calm but I was livid inside. I went into Mr. Belali's office and told him about it. He advised me to go home, take a rest and come and see him in the morning when he would discuss it with me.

I don't like coincidences and it seemed a bit odd that he waited until I was leaving until he came back at me. I'd read a book called *The Celestine Prophecy* which opened my eyes towards coincidence. The author claimed there was no such thing and everything has a meaning. Like you think about someone you haven't seen for years and suddenly you get a call or meet them. Coincidences have a reason, and I thought Saud had been keeping tabs on me ever since I'd come back nearly two years ago.

I went home and slept erratically that night, worrying about getting home again. I had the lost dream again. I didn't need all that again. The next day I passed by Mr. Belali's office and he called me in. I sat and had tea with him. He dropped a bombshell on me. He told me he and Mr. Rebdi had paid Saud the money before I arrived. Nick had persuaded them I was worth it, that he needed me to get the dealerships and I could help with managing the office while he was out with clients. They had agreed after talking to Saud and he had written the letter I carried with me. Blimey, I didn't realise I owed them now. He explained they wouldn't be asking for it back as I'd earnt their trust by managing their company for the last eighteen months.

'If he comes back, send him in to us and we will deal with him. You don't owe Saud Al-Harbi any money, he's had it,' he said.

'Thank you, I was worried he would block my exit again,' I said.

'You can go home then your life can revert to normal in your terms,' he said. But I knew it wouldn't, not for a long time if ever, and so in a sense did Mr. Belali.

***

Phew, what a relief. I realised I might actually get home without any problems this time.

Mr Basi did come back and I was glad I didn't have to deal with him again. Mr. Belali sent him away with a flea in his ear and he was really angry that Saud had lied to him. He'd thought he could intimidate me and scare me into paying him.

This new feeling of being trusted gave me confidence and I enjoyed my last few months at work.

The team organised an office party when I was leaving. Everyone had been brought back from the respective offices and they had made food and bought drinks. The conference room was decorated and each one had signed a massive wall chart. We took photos with everyone sitting on the floor in the main office and I was given an engraved Mont Blanc pen. I was invited to three weddings in India and Mac's wife asked me to come and stay with them in the Philippians for a holiday. I was so emotional it brought tears to my eyes.

***

When I got home another whirlwind hit me, but that's another story. You don't want to know about that, maybe another time. At least I'd learnt to cook and I was going to need to.

Acknowledgements

A big thank you goes to David Brown, who got me into this mess and helped create this story.

I would like to thank everyone who read the manuscript and offered suggestions for improvements, in particular my three children Emma, Matthew and Jonathan, and their mum who looked after them while I was away. A massive thank you to my wife Sharon who has put up with me spending every spare moment writing it. There are also many others to thank for their support, their reminders and memories of the time, plus the people who heard the story and prompted me to write about it. It's been fun writing it, and looking back, all the problems have become amusing.

Any mistakes, it goes without saying, are entirely my own.

Lightning Source UK Ltd.
Milton Keynes UK
UKHW01f1819110518
322489UK00001B/225/P